PRACTICAL SELF-RELIANCE

Reducing Your Dependency On Others

John D. McCann

ISBN-978-0-9905006-0-5

Being Self-Reliant is not a pastime,
but a way of life

John D. McCann

The best place to find a helping hand is
at the end of your own arm.

Swedish Proverb

A person who's reliant on others for the necessities of life
will always be subject to the people, companies, and
agencies who feed, house, and protect him.

Steven Gregersen

If an American is to amount to anything he must rely
upon himself, and not upon the state; he must take pride
in his own work, instead of sitting idle to envy the luck
of others. He must face life with resolute courage, win
victory if he can, and accept defeat if he must, without
seeking to place on his fellow man a responsibility which
is not theirs.

Theodore Roosevelt

TABLE OF CONTENTS

<u>DEDICATION</u>

As always, I dedicate this book to my wonderful wife
Denise. She is my best friend and partner in self-reliance. She is
skilled in so many things and yet is the most humble person I
know. She is truly treasured in my life and I appreciate that she
has chosen me to share her life with.

ACKNOWLEDGEMENTS

First, I would like to acknowledge my parents. Although they are both gone now, they taught me more than they will ever know, and instilled in me a love of, and desire for, self-reliance. Having survived both, the great depression, and World War II, their life after the war was dedicated to getting a piece of land in the country and being as self-reliant as they could. After building a house from a shack, growing a garden, raising rabbits and chickens, they were ready for children. For that to happen they had to adopt and I, fortunately, am the beneficiary of that kind act. I owe them a debt of gratitude for having given me a life with a loving family, and a passion for doing things myself. I miss them.

I would like to thank Steve and Susan Gregersen for their friendship. They have been more that helpful when it came to providing some of the photos for this book, as well as advice. Although they both live a self-reliant lifestyle on a homestead in Montana, they both write books and have time for friends, as evidenced by Steve also providing the Foreword to this book. They are truly gracious, honest, and wise people and I respect what they have accomplished.

Christopher Nyerges has also provided a helping hand and some of his photos will also be found here. He has lived and taught self-reliance since the early 1970's and written many books on the subject. I am fortunate to have him as a friend.

Last, but not least, I must acknowledge my good friend Jim Tompkins. He is truly a work of art and lives the self-reliant lifestyle in every way. We spend most of our time together either doing, or discussing, self-reliance and survival. He is unequivocally unique.

FOREWORD

Too many people think in an "all or nothing" frame of mind. We live completely off the grid on a twenty-acre, (almost!) self-sufficient homestead in the mountains of northwestern, Montana. We get inquiries from people who want to be more self-reliant yet don't want to live as we do. Often it's just impractical for some very valid reasons, to leave their present location to buy some raw land and start all over again.

The truth of the matter is that living a self-reliant life does not require a remote location. There are already a lot of things they can do to become more self-reliant right where they live and work and in this book John tells them (and you!) how to do it.

My wife and I first met John McCann and his wife Denise at a self-reliance event being held in Wyoming. I'll never forget him looking me in the eye and asking what I thought of solar stills for acquiring water. I completely misread him, thinking he was one of those people who thought solar stills were a good way to get water so I bit my lip before answering in as diplomatic way as possible that, "in my experience I wasn't very impressed with them." I was surprised when he completely agreed with me and we began talking about people who promote things they've never actually tried.

That told me some things about John McCann. First, don't try to pull the wool over his eyes. He has little patience with pretenders. Second, he is the type that isn't going to blindly take anyone's word on a subject, so if he says it works or doesn't work, it's because he's tried it himself.

Since then I've had the chance to read his books and articles and to be in classes he's taught. We've spent time getting to know each other better and each encounter left me with a greater admiration and respect for his integrity and teaching abilities.

John has put that integrity and his teaching abilities to work in this book that's full of ideas you can use to become more self-reliant right where you live. The truth is that you don't need twenty, secluded, mountain acres in the forests of northwestern, Montana to become more self-reliant. You just need motivation, determination and knowledge.

The knowledge you'll need is in John's book. You're on your own for motivation and determination.

Some things we buy are an expense. Others are an investment. This book is definitely an investment.

Steven Gregersen
Author of
Creating the Low-Budget Homestead
The Greenhorn's Guide to Chainsaws and Firewood Cutting
The Beginner's Guide to Reloading Ammunition
The Gun Guide For Those Who Know Nothing About Firearms

Chapter 1
__INTRODUCTION__

I was born in the 1950's and self-reliance was a way of life. Most families, at least in my area, had the means to take care of their basic needs. They gardened, preserved food, repaired their clothes, homes, and vehicles. It was the way we lived, and we didn't depend on others for all our needs. Of course, we were not totally self-reliant, but then we didn't wish to be. We had to depend on others for various aspects of our needs. But we tried to limit those dependencies. Anything we could do ourselves, reduced those things we had to buy, or pay others to do.

Society has changed since that time and many people have become almost totally dependent on others for their daily needs. When something stops working, it is thrown away, not repaired. Some of this is a result of products being inferior, and designed to be replaced often. But for some, it is a case of being easier to just go and buy another. Food not eaten is normally disposed of, instead of saved for a future meal; what we called "left-overs." When I was a kid, everybody had patches on their jeans, especially the knees. Yet today, clothes are rarely repaired, and are thrown in the garbage.

I see many people today go about their lives with most everything taken care of by others. The majority don't even think about self-reliance. It takes effort and is often an inconvenience. Much of the food purchased is pre-prepared, all repairs and maintenance are done by others, they possess few skills outside of the expertise required for their job, and recreation and media are omnipotent. They will often tell you, they have little time to take care of their own needs.

Self-Reliance vs. Self-Sufficiency

In my opinion, self-reliance is being able to do as much as we can without outside assistance. It means reliance on oneself, or one's own abilities, skills, efforts, resources, etc., as opposed to those of others or external sources. An example might be that a city dweller might not be able to grow their own grain, but they can buy grain and grind it themselves. Everything a person can do to eliminate an outside source will make a person more self-reliant.

On the other hand, Self-Sufficiency is the ability to maintain oneself without outside aid, being able to provide for all of one's needs. Unfortunately, in today's world, we must live with a dependence or inter-dependence on others. In the pioneer days people could not produce everything they needed and had to rely on others for supplies they could not furnish. Even mountain men went to rendezvous' in order to sell their furs and purchase needed supplies. They were both very self-reliant, but not self-sufficient

It is even more difficult today to provide for all our needs. You can use solar panels to help you provide some of your own electric power, but you can't manufacture those panels. The same with the batteries you use to store that energy. You can buy a vehicle that is more fuel efficient, but you must still rely on somebody to provide that fuel, or somebody to provide you with the ingredients to make your own. If you have an electric car, somebody must provide the power to produce the electricity to recharge it. Therefore we must depend on other sources for those needs we cannot provide for ourselves.

The bottom line, in my opinion, it would be nearly impossible for anyone to be truly self-sufficient today. But everything we can learn to do for ourselves, which precludes us from depending on others, moves us that much closer to self-reliance.

What This Book Isn't

It seems like every day there is a new book on prepping for, or bugging out from, an upcoming Armageddon, or an End of the World as We Know It situation. That is not the intent of this book.

This book is not about Homesteading or Living Off -The-Grid, although some of the information provided here would assist in those endeavors. Nor is this book on Emergency Preparedness, per se, but essentially the more self-reliant you become, the better you will be able to react to, and deal with, an emergency situation.

What This Book Is

The intention of this book is not to make you totally self-reliant, as that is impractical and unrealistic. But, in the alternative, it should provide you with practical self-reliance information that can be used by anyone, no matter your location, financial situation, or depth in which you wish to be involved. You also don't have to run off to the woods or a ranch to be self-reliant. Even though you don't live out on acres of land, or have decided that homesteading is not for you, you can still practice various aspects of self-reliance.

Whether you live in a city, an apartment, the suburbs, the country, or elsewhere, the information provided here can help you be more self-reliant, and therefore less dependent on others for your needs. Of course, it is better if you have just a small plot of land, but for those who don't, you will just have to improvise more. I have tried to provide information of various levels so you can have practical ideas to assist you in doing so.

Some information I will provide in detail, while other information will be cursory as an in depth study would be better accomplished from information found in sources that deal directly with that subject. For example, I will not delve deeply into having or raising animals or livestock. This is an area that is beyond the scope of this book and would be better studied from a publication, or persons, that deal exclusively with that subject. However, I will often provide my thoughts on those subjects. This book will not address all aspects of self-reliance, but those anyone could attempt, most anywhere. I try to provide some realistic options for the various subjects addressed. This will allow the reader to come away with actual solutions that have been tried by myself, or by friends and associates, and have been proven effective or beneficial for the purpose of self-reliance.

Living in a city or apartment does not preclude you from being self-reliant. These are green peppers being grown in an old recycle bin on a porch. They could be on a roof or a balcony.

Needs vs. Wants

Self-Reliance is a different lifestyle than many people are accustomed to, and requires a willingness to look at things differently. There will be those people who view your actions as needy or give the impression that you are stingy, as opposed to prudent. Others are more concerned with what others might think about them, instead of being proud of what they are doing. I once knew a couple who always threw their empty soda and beer cans in the garbage. I asked why they did that instead of recycling them. The husband stated, "I am a professional and how would it look if someone saw me standing in front of a recycle machine pushing in old cans like some derelict." Apparently, the need to look affluent was more important to them than the need to recycle.

I know of various families in my area that have all the toys, such as ATV's and snowmobiles. One family lives in an old trailer that always seems to be falling down around them and another an old house in disrepair. Both of these families have a nice piece of land in the country, but neither of them garden. They have the toys; one even has a dirt-track stock car for racing, but these toys require them to be more dependent on others. They seem to have little regard for being self-reliant and more concerned with those things that are fun, even if those things make them more dependent on others. We all need recreation, but at what cost?

Keep in mind that in order to be more self-reliant, you might need to examine those things in your life that you need, as opposed to those things that you want. Often, they will not be the same. You might look at an item differently if you try to determine if it is something that will help you be more independent, as opposed to more dependent, on someone or something else. If something will merely place you further in a position of dependency, it might better be substituted for something that won't. Some decisions will not be easy.

In Summary

Don't fool yourself, self-reliance takes time, effort, and a willingness not to take the easy way out. But it provides you with a sense of independence and the pride associated with taking care of your own needs, if only some of them.

I recall having been without power for five days and a neighbor asking me how I was doing. Kidding, I asked, "Why, did something happen." The reality of the situation was that my wife and I had been merely inconvenienced and had gone on about our lives the previous few days, having all that we needed. I also recall a snow storm where many trees and most power lines went down and people could not get out of their homes as most roads were closed. On the second day, we heard on the radio that some people were indicating that they were in "dire" need of food and supplies. The County was contemplating dropping in supplies by helicopter. I could not believe that in two days people were out of food and supplies and in "dire need." Certainly, they were not self-reliant people.

Everybody can have some degree of self-reliance if they want to. But they must have a desire to do so. Again, nobody can expect to become totally self-reliant, but the more you do for yourself, the more you will trade dependence for independence. I hope that this book provides you with some ideas that will assist you in working towards that goal.

PART 1
FOOD IS NECESSARY

Chapter 2
<u>Obtaining Food</u>

For most people, when they want food, they go to the nearest grocery store and buy what they need. However, grocery stores are not a dependable source for a self-reliant person. When I was sixteen, I worked evenings at a large grocery store restocking shelves, as they had an area in the back with additional supplies.

Those days are gone and today, what you see is what they have. Have you ever heard a large storm is heading your way and when you get to the grocery store the milk, eggs, and bread are either gone, or nearly gone, as well as many other essentials. If you cannot depend on a grocery store for your needs when there is a storm brewing, think what would happen if a real emergency situation occurred over an extended time period.

For the self-reliant person, having a supply of food is just a normal way of life. If you do shop at a grocery store, always purchase more than you need. If you need a can of beans, buy several and store the extras. Of course, the same goes with other items as well.

But keep in mind that depending on a grocery store is not a prudent strategy for self-reliance. In this chapter we will discuss various ways you can obtain the food you need. We will start with gardening, which is a way that you can provide food for yourself, without relying on others. Although I will discuss this important issue, and provide recommendations, a complete guide on how to garden is beyond the scope of this book.

For those that absolutely can't garden, or don't have the space, many alternative options will be discussed such as Community Gardening, Foraging, Farmer's Markets, Co-Ops, and

CSA's . The chapter will end with a brief discussion about Raising Livestock, Keeping Bees, Fishing, Hunting and Trapping.

Gardening For Food

Gardening is a way that you can provide food for yourself, without relying on others, with the bonus that it will be fresher and more nutritious than anything you can buy. I don't intend to cover gardening in such depth that you will be able to use this as a gardening reference guide, but hope to show that just about anybody can grow at least a little food, and hopefully provide some ideas to get you started.

Even if you have limited space, gardening is an option for obtaining food. Every little bit you can provide for yourself is less you must rely on someone else for. I've heard people say that they just don't have any room.

If you live in an apartment, or have limited space, you may not be able to have a full blown garden, but you should be able to grow some vegetables The secret is utilizing the space you have to grow what you can. For people who may only have a balcony, or small porch, container gardening is an option. Using containers to grow vegetables allows you to move them around, if needed, and provides you with something Even though I have over an acre of land, and a good size garden at the back of my property, I still utilize container gardening so we have some vegetables close to the kitchen which include lettuce, herbs, and tomatoes.

Containers for container gardens can be purchased for the purpose, but there are many different types of containers that can be easily recycled for this purpose. I have used old five gallon buckets, old spackle pails, small garbage cans, and one that always reminds me of recycling, an old recycle bin provided free by a previous garbage company (see photo in Chapter One -

Introduction). Containers can be used on balconies, decks, porches, and even in your yard. They allow you to grow food in minimum space and keep it close for easy pickings.

Cherry tomatoes growing inside an old spackle bucket alongside a back porch making for easy pickings. This could be kept on the balcony of an apartment in the city.

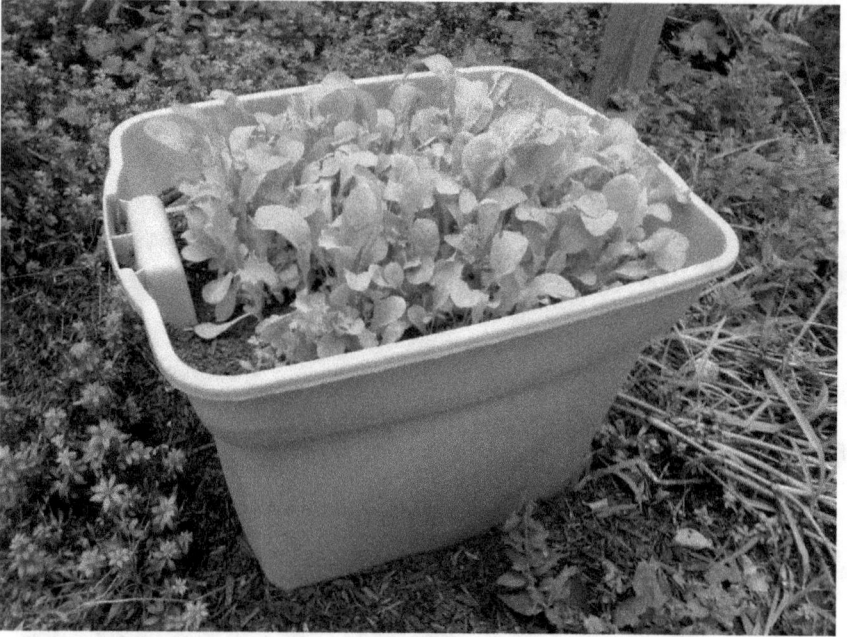

Lettuce growing in a large plastic been sitting in the landscaping outside of a screened in porch

Green peppers being grown on a patio in an old recycle bin.

This photo shows that living in an urban area does not preclude you from having a small garden. Here is Barry King in Sabadell, Spain, starting his garden on his balcony. Photo by Orquidea King

When space is a constraint also consider growing up, not out. Planting vegetables that grow on vines, like pole beans and cucumbers, allows you to grow plants vertically up a few poles or a trellis, which uses less space for a given plant. This works well for any size garden but is especially prudent when you have limited room.

Sometimes having a garden is not a matter of space, but regulation. I have a friend, Antone Andrade, who lives in a duplex in the suburbs and has a decent size yard. Unfortunately, his lease precludes him from digging up the lawn or even placing a raised bed on the lawn. He was determined to have a garden so he built a raised bed on legs so it would not sit directly on the lawn. He was able to fulfill the requirements of the lease and still have a garden.

This is a raised bed built by Antone Andrade in order to comply with his lease agreement which does not permit raised beds directly on the ground. Photo by Antone Andrade

Even if you do have space, conserving space can sometimes be an advantage. The "Three Sisters" is a way to grow three different vegetables in one space. The early Europeans might have never survived if the gift of the Three Sisters had not been received from the Native Americans.

The Three Sisters incorporates corn, beans, and squash. Corn is planted on small mounds which provides a natural pole for the vines of the beans to climb up. The beans convert energy into nitrogen filled nodules on their roots. As the beans grow, they use the stored nitrogen as food, as well as provide nitrogen to the soil for use by the corn the following year. The squash is planted around the corn and acts as a living mulch, both shading the soil from emerging weeds and keeping it cool and moist. It should be noted that in order for proper corn pollination an area of at least ten feet by ten feet be used for the Three Sisters.

Before leaving container gardening I would also like to address composting. This is a great way to add nutrient-rich humus to your garden, which fuels plant growth, and restores vitality to depleted soil.

Even a small compost bin can provide you with nutrient-rich humus for a garden of any size. Photo by Susan Gregersen

The size of your compost bin will be determined by how much space you have, and a smaller sized bin can fit on even the smallest property. If you live where you have absolutely no yard, then composting probably won't be an option.

If you do have some property, a large compost bin will provide you with plenty of rich humus for your garden. This is a large, three section, compost bin built by the author.

As you can see, even a little space will allow you to grow at least some of your own food. But what if you absolutely don't have any room? Let's look at some options.

Community Gardening

In the past, community gardens were a way to provide food during war or depression. During World War II they were called "Victory" gardens. However, today they are often used in urban areas in order to rejuvenate old abandoned or vacant lots, and at the same time, provide a place for members of the community to grow a garden.

The above two photos show examples of community gardens where members can have small plots to plant their own garden
Photos by Christopher Nyerges

Community gardens are normally run and maintained by the gardeners who actively participate. Some of these gardens have one big garden that everyone works on together, and in others, each participating member gets an individual plot of a specific size. Normally there is some type of fee to be part of the garden and some form of management organization.

If you have no place to garden on your own property this might be a viable option and a way for you to grow some of your own vegetables. Of course you will have to check out your local area to see if any community gardens exist, or possibly you could start one. The first step is always finding the plot of land and getting permission to use it.

In Switzerland, , where my wife is from, most apartment and condo complexes provide a small plot of gardening space for each unit, and the price is included in the rent or mortgage. The last time we were over there, my wife's brother asked us over for dinner and all the vegetables came from their small garden..

Foraging For Wild Edibles

The foraging for wild edibles doesn't sound like a viable means in which to gather real food, but don't fool yourself. I have two friends that actually forage for wild edibles in order to supply them to restaurants, as well as farmers markets. Wild edibles are not limited to the country, and can be found in the city in vacant lots as well as in your own yard.

With that being said, I would first like to state you must know what you are looking for and you should NEVER pick and eat a plant that you have not 100% identified as edible. There are many reference books and field guides which can help in the identification of edible plants. I also suggest a plant walk with an expert to help in the correct identification. On the east coast I recommend Wildman Steve Brill, and on the west coast, Christopher Nyerges. It should also be noted that many survival manuals regurgitate the old "universal edibility test" from old military manuals. It recommends putting a small amount of a plant in your mouth and wait to see what happens. If you do this with poison hemlock, which grows everywhere around my area, you might not have to wait long... it will kill you.

In order to illustrate the abundance of edible plants you can find, even in your own yard, the following is extracted from an article I wrote, called "Weeds Can Feed." For the complete article with more plants and photos, check out the "Useful Plants" section under articles at www.SurvivalResources.com

When we have guests over for dinner, we usually like to start the meal with a salad. When the salad is placed on the table, and after a bewildered look by our guests, we are normally informed that the salad looks splendid, but then asked what is in it. Our salads seldom resemble the usual mixture of lettuces and greens presented at your normal table and are often full of color. Yet the contents are rarely identifiable by the ordinary diner. I usually retort that the contents are merely weeds and that the main course will probably contain more. Although surprised at the outset, before the salad is completed, compliments from delicious to an epicurean's delight, gush forth from the guests.

Most people just don't realize the plethora of weeds around their yard that are edible, healthy, and delectable. Weeds are often pulled up around the yard and garden as a nuisance without realizing they can be as healthy and delicious as the vegetables grown in the garden. And best of all, weeds are free for the taking. So let's examine some of those weeds that can feed in the Northeast, where we reside.

In the early spring, you have the young Dandelion greens. The leaves of the dandelion are so toothed that it got its name from the French which means "lions tooth." Dandelions are well known, and usually dreaded, as the fuzzy headed yellow plant, that tends to take over your lawn. But in the early spring, before they form those pinnacles of yellow flowers, and are still in the small rosette of leaves stage, they are not yet too bitter to eat. At this time, the small leaves, especially the pale whitish portion just below the soil, can be a great addition to salads. Add a little olive oil, lemon juice, and a pinch of salt. As a potherb, these young leaves can also be boiled or steamed for 5-10 minutes. Either way, they are full of vitamins A & C. However, they do cook down, so collect plenty if you are using them as a potherb.

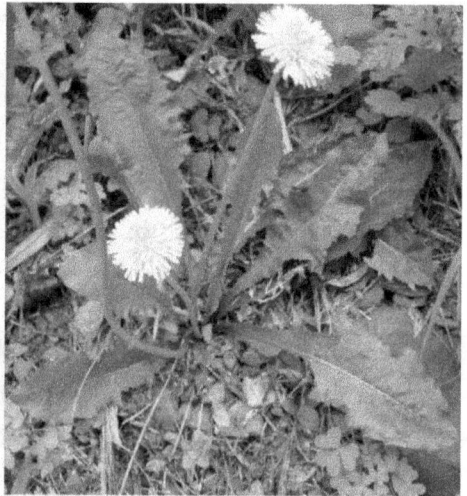

The left photo shows a close-up of a Dandelion flower and the right photo shows the entire plant

As the season progresses, and the flowers appear, dandelions become too bitter to eat. However, you can still use the yellow flower heads by dipping them in batter and deep frying them, like a fritter. As a last resort, you can bake the roots until brown and then grind them for use as you would any commercial coffee. Although a little bitter, it can be used as a coffee extender in an emergency situation, by mixing it with your commercial blend.

The Common Chickweed is another weed that appears everywhere and can be eaten all year long. If you remember where it grows, you can even find it growing under the snow in the winter, and harvest it for consumption. A small plant, normally laying flat on the ground, has a flower so small it normally goes unnoticed. Yet, if one was to examine it closely they would discern that the miniature flower is notched so deeply that it appears to have ten petals as opposed to its actual five. Common chickweed makes a nice addition to a salad and can be boiled or steamed for about five minutes for use as a potherb.

Common Chickweed can be found most anywhere around a yard, vacant lots, etc., and is a great addition to a salad.

An often overlooked weed is Purslane, which to the chagrin of many, grows well in every garden (although you didn't plant it there) and many other areas around the yard. It is a smooth prostrate plant with reddish-green stems, with small paddle-shaped leaves. It has leaves and stems that have a sweet-sour flavor and are mucilaginous. They are rich in vitamins A & C as well as calcium and phosphorus. They make a great addition to a salad raw and can also be cooked and pickled. The seeds can be used as well to make a nutritious flour.

Purslane with its paddle shaped leaves and reddish green stems.

Once salad is completed, there is an abundance of other weeds that just keep filling our pots with steamed or boiled greens.

In the spring, we can't wait for the Ostrich Fern Fiddleheads. Still all curled up at the heads, they are great steamed. And don't forget to leave some of the stems attached, as they taste as good as the fiddleheads. Unfortunately, once they uncurl, they become poisonous, so enjoy them when you can.

Fiddleheads of the Ostrich Fern ready to pick and ready to cook.

Although I recommend wearing gloves for picking Stinging Nettles, once they are boiled or steamed, they lose their sting. A Great potherb!

The Stinging Nettle is an excellent pot herb. Nettles have little stinging hairs on the stems and the leaves, so use caution when harvesting them. Gloves are recommended, and either keep your arms and wrists covered, or avoid having the plant rub on either. The Stinging Nettle has leaves that are coarsely toothed and are in opposite pairs every few inches on the upper portion of the stalk. The leaves are ovate to lanceolate in shape and usually have a heart-shaped base. Small greenish flowers appear in small, branching clusters, from the leaf axils. In the spring you can pick the upper two or three pairs of leaves, but by summer I recommend only the upper two. As a steamed or boiled potherb, it doesn't get much better than Stinging Nettle, and as soon as they are cooked, the stinging properties disappear.

Lamb's Quarters, also known as Goosefoot (because the leaves remind some of a goose's foot) and Pigweed, it is both, a weed that can be used raw in salads, or cooked as a potherb, and they are delicious both ways. The leaves, which get up to four inches long, are somewhat diamond shaped when mature and broadly toothed. They grow alternately from the stalk on petioles about half the length of the leaf. Although they are a dark bluish-green color on the top, the underside is usually covered with a whitish-gray powder. The small, upper most leaves on mature plants have more of a lanceolate shape and lack teeth on their margins.

Lamb's Quarter is a good potherb that grows almost everywhere.

Closely related to spinach, Lamb's Quarters can be eaten from spring through fall. In the spring, until the plant reaches up to twelve inches, you can normally use the entire plant as a cooked potherb. The tender upper leaves are great as an addition to a salad. As the plant gets larger, select the upper more tender leaves for cooking. Again, they really cook down, so pick a lot. It should also be noted that the Lamb's Quarters little black seeds, available in late fall, can be boiled and used to make a breakfast type gruel, or ground into flour. They are very nutritious.

Again, this is just a sampling of the weeds that are available for the taking and provide nutritious food. If you are interested in more weeds that feed for free, see the article mentioned at the beginning of this section.

A view of a Yellow Morel with its brain looking cap.

There are other edibles that can be found in the field and even the woods. In the spring I can't wait for the morels, which is the only mushroom I collect and eat. Many mushrooms can be poisonous and we had a local instructor die after eating one that he misidentified.

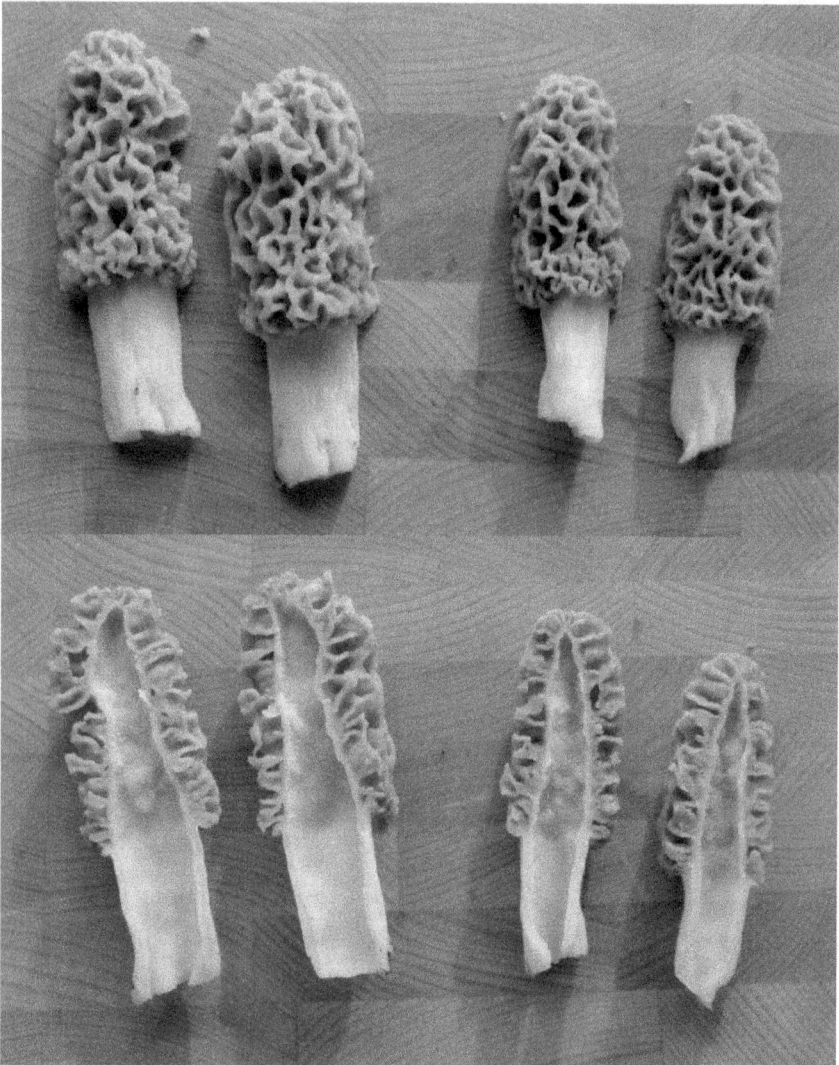

The top photo shows the outside of the yellow morel which have been cut in half lengthwise. The bottom photo shows the inside of the yellow morel.

Morels come out in the spring about two to three weeks after the last frost. Temperature is the key and they are usually located on south or west facing slopes or on flat areas between tree canopies. Morels feed on the decay of a dying tree and can often be found the year after an area has been burned.

First of all, if you are going to pick Morels, make sure you identify them correctly. In my area, we have the gray and yellow Morel, and they are pretty easy to identify. To me, they look like a brain, but others think they look like a sponge. They have a hollow stem and the inside looks like a chocolate Santa, and the hood is all one piece with the stem; not a separate piece. However, make sure that you absolutely identify them before eating them. There are "false morels" and they will make you sick. If you cut them lengthwise, they will not have hollow stems like the morel.

When collected, morels should be carried in a mesh bag in order to allow them to release their spore back into the environment for future reproduction. Morels are great sautéed, after being cleaned, and can be stored fresh in a refrigerator for up to two weeks when cleaned and prepared properly. This is not meant to be an identification guide for morels, or other mushrooms, and if you are interested, I suggest you get the book "Morel Hunting" by John and Theresa Maybrier, and get some instruction from an expert on the subject who can personally show you.

If you are going to become involved with foraging, again I suggest you get some instruction from someone with knowledge. I would recommend Christopher Nyerges on the west coast and "Wildman" Steve Brill on the east coast. Of course, there are others. Some books I would recommend for identifying edible plants and their uses are: "Peterson's Edible Wild Plants" by Lee Allen Peterson, "Guide To Wild Foods and Useful Plants" by Christopher Nyerges, "The Forager's Harvest" & "Nature's Garden" by Samuel Thayer, "Identifying and Harvesting Edible

and Medicinal Plants" by "Wildman" Steve Brill, and Northeast
Foraging by Leda Meredith..

Farmers Markets

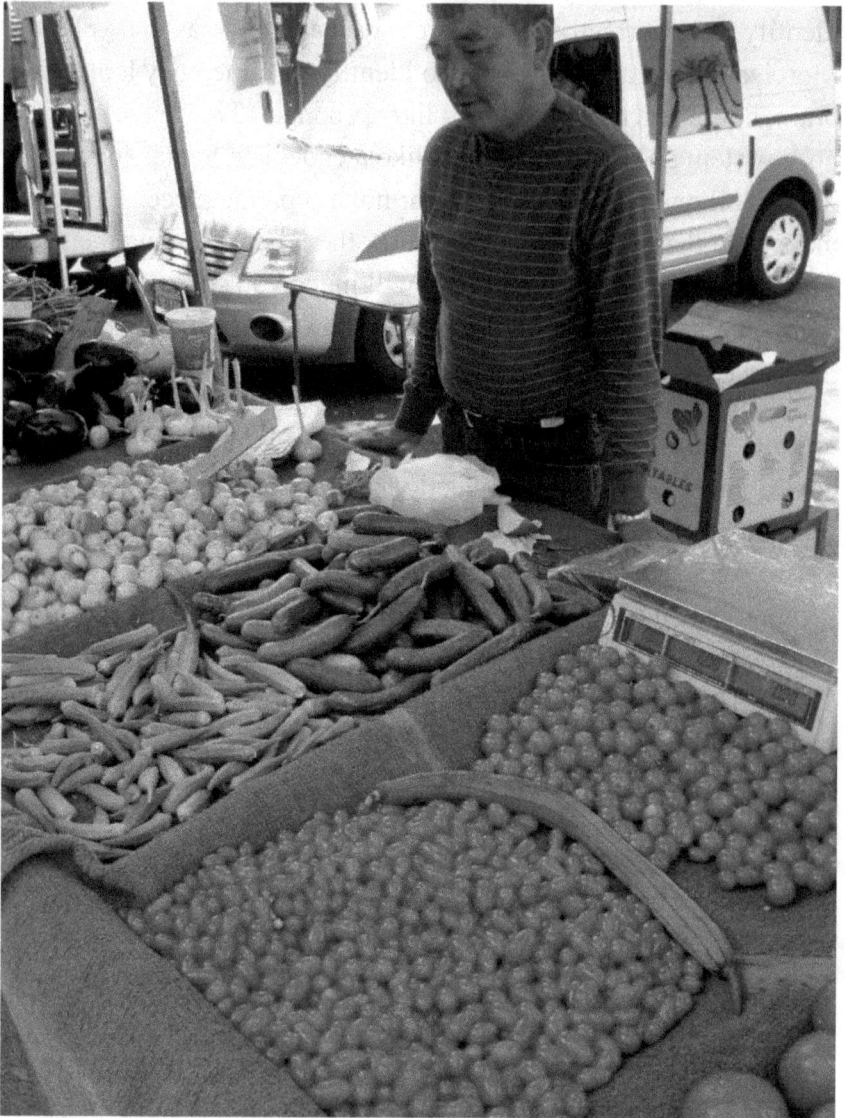

**A Farmers Market is a great place to buy fresh produce directly
from farmers.** Photo by Christopher Nyerges

If you cannot plant and grow your own vegetables, then a farmers market is a place where you can get fresh produce from farmers who sell directly to consumers. They are a great place to obtain fresh vegetables, eggs, cheeses, hand harvested honey, and other small-batch foodstuffs.

Even if you can grow a small amount of your own vegetables, a farmers market is a great place to go to buy extra for dehydrating and canning, which will be discussed in the next chapter. It is also an advantage as farmers can get a good price, not having to go through a middleman, and you, the consumer, get the freshest products at a reasonable price. It also provides a place for farmers and consumers to meet, develop relationships, and exchange information.

Food Co-Ops & CSA's

These are further options for those who cannot grow their own food. Food Cooperatives are like a retail store that is owned by the workers and customers. They provide high quality food at the best value for its members. It is an alternative for fresh and locally grown food, yet provides the convenience of a normal grocery store. Some are run like actual retail stores and some are like buying clubs. Food Co-Ops will often support the local farmers of a community.

A CSA stands for "Community Supported Agriculture" and provides residents of a city another means to obtain fresh produce grown locally by farmers. You must be a member of a CSA, and basically you are buying a "share" of vegetables from a farmer. That produce is then delivered to a specified location in the neighborhood. Members must pay for an entire season upfront. Some CSA's also offer, for an additional cost, fruit, eggs, meat, etc. For more information check your local area.

Raising Livestock

Raising animals for food is another activity that almost anybody can become involved in, except for those in an inner city or housing which has regulations against it. The first thing I'd like to mention, if you are thinking about raising animals, is they require care and they tie you down. If you are the type who travels often, then you will need someone who can feed and care for the animals. They are not a part-time activity. You will also need to check with local ordinances to ensure it is legal to do so in your area.

Obviously, the smaller your property, the smaller the animals you will be able to maintain. However, chickens and rabbits can be raised with very little room. Chickens can provide eggs, fertilizer for your garden, and of course, meat. Some areas will allow residents to raise chicken, but not roosters, because of the noise. You can still have eggs, you just won't be able to fertilize the eggs to raise more chickens.

Rabbits take up the least amount of room, are inexpensive to feed, and can be raised just for the purpose of using their droppings for fertilizing your garden. It is very high in nitrogen and phosphorus, both of which are necessary for the soil in a garden. Many people raise rabbits for that purpose alone. I know of one individual who built his rabbit coop over his compost bin (we will discuss composting in Chapter 8), so the rabbit droppings fell directly into the compost.

Rabbits can also be raised for meat, which is high in protein. If you raise angora rabbits, the hair can be used for knitting.

The larger your property, the larger the animals you can sustain. Pigs can be raised for meat and goats, and cattle can be raised for both meat and dairy. Again, animals take time and care, and the larger the animal, the more expensive it is to maintain it.

Keeping Bees

Raising bees is another means in which a self-reliant person can obtain food, with the added benefit of making bees wax to make candles, and at the same time they also will pollinate your garden. Honey stores forever and never rots, so it always remains edible. It also has medicinal uses.

Bee Keeping does require some specialized equipment but can provide you with honey, and more. Photo by Jim Thmpkins

Bee hives take up very little room and even people in the city have raised bees on a roof or balcony. A bee hive can produce up to fifty pounds of honey in a season, and that's a lot of honey. Of course, you will need some specialized equipment to start and maintain a bee hive, and it is complicated enough that you will want to study before starting, and get involved with some people who have already raised bees, and learn from them.

Fishing

Fishing is another means of which you can obtain food. It can be an occasional effort, or a sustained effort, depending on your local resources. My father was an avid weekend fisherman and we always had plenty of fish, both fresh to eat, and frozen for later. We would often share with neighbors, as my father was quite proficient.

There are people in areas like Alaska that actually depend on salmon for a large portion of their winter food, but most people use fishing as a supplemental source of food, not primary. Again, it depends on your location, resources, and ability to fish.

Hunting & Trapping

Hunting and Trapping are a means in which to obtain meat. It is an activity that requires some skill, training, and equipment to be successful. For some, it is a way to supplement their food supplies, while for others, it is their major source of meat. Like those who raise animals for food, you must be willing to kill the animal and have the knowledge to butcher the meat and process it for future use. Preserving might include freezing, smoking, or canning the meat.

As with some of the other subjects discussed, the hunting and trapping for food is beyond the scope of this book. If you are interested in this for a means of gathering food there is a lot of information available. I would suggest that you find someone who has a high skill level and learn from them.

Chapter 3

<u>Food Preservation</u>

A search for ways to preserve food has been an activity since earliest history. Drying herbs, meat, and fish was the earliest method. Then, in the 1800's, the development of using heat in a sealed container allowed food to be preserved in cans and glass jars. Unfortunately, with the advent of modern refrigeration, and especially the convenience of a refrigerator in every home, and pre-packaged food on the shelves of stores, many people have stopped thinking about preserving their own food today.

But for the purpose of self reliance, the ability to preserve the fresh food you grow, harvest, raise, kill, or obtain by other means is an important skill. We have examined the various ways to obtain food, so let's discuss the different ways we can preserve food so that it will last longer for our needs.

It should be noted, that although we will identify and discuss numerous preservation methods, this is not meant to be a tutorial on the intricacies of those methods involved. Each area will be discussed in a generalized manner whereby you can decide if that method is best for your needs. There are plenty of books available, that are dedicated to this subject, and some will be provided under the appropriate headings below.

Air Drying Herbs

One of the easiest foods to preserve are herbs. We grow a lot of herbs and, although we use many fresh, we dry enough to get us through the winter and spring of the following season. Although we have been known to dry some in a dehydrator, most we air dry. Also, with the air drying method of preservation, you aren't effected when the power goes out!,

Air drying is very simple because, unlike fruits and vegetables which require very low humidity for safe drying, you don't have that concern with herbs, . You simply pick your herbs early in the morning, before it gets hot, but after the dew dries. This is when the oils that provide the fragrance and flavor are at their maximum. When you wait for the heat of the day, much of this oil returns to the roots.

Once you pick the herbs, making sure you leave adequate stems attached, you simply tie them in small bundles by the stems, using string or other small cordage. Hang them upside down in a warm and dry place out of direct sunlight We usually hang the bundles in our potting shed and in the garage, up towards the rafters where it is warm. Keep the bundles small and lose and leave enough room between the bundles for air to circulate around them.

A view of oregano hanging to dry in the author's potting shed.

It is that easy. It should only take a couple of days and you will know they are sufficiently dry when they become brittle and crumble when you touch them. Simply strip the leaves from the stems and store them in jars in a dark cabinet, as exposure to light will degrade the flavor.

Dehydrating

The oldest method of food preservation is dehydration. For centuries people dried food using the sun and wind, or the smoke of a fire. Unfortunately, your days were limited by the weather.

Unlike canning, which we will discuss next, dehydrating is basically drying food in order to remove the moisture which inhibits the growth of microorganisms and bacteria. Because you are simply removing water, dehydrating food is a cheap and easy way to preserve food. It also allows for longer storage terms. Dehydrated food is also very light weight and takes up much less room for storage than canned food.

There are many different commercial dehydrators available on the market today. They can range from $30 - $50.00 for the smaller round designed types, to $200 - $300 for the larger high end front loading units. The better units have fans at the back or side providing more even air circulation and, unlike the round units that have a fan at the bottom, you don't have to worry about liquid that might drip down from the food being dried.

I have found that the smaller units are fine for the occasional or small dehydrating needs, but if you get serious and dehydrate often, or a lot of food, the larger front loading units are worth the extra money. I've had an old American Harvest round type dehydrator for over twenty years and it still works fine for small jobs. I also have an Excalibur nine tray unit, and it has served us well. We have used it to dry food on the trays, and have even taken out all the trays except the top one, and hung herbs from the top rack for drying. I also like the fact that the unit has a drying guide on the top which tells you which temperature setting to use for a specific food being dehydrated.

Parsley shown on trays after having been dried in the dehydrator.

I should mention that dehydrating requires that you use various temperatures at varying lengths of time to adequately dehydrate the food. I highly recommend that you get a guide that provides this information. One of the books I use is *Making & Using Dried Foods* by Phyllis Hobson. She provides an excellent guide to include pretreating methods, and temperature and length of time to dry for various specific fruits, vegetables, herbs, meats, dairy, and grains. Various recipes are also included. I highly recommend this book

This is a view of bundles of mint being dried by hanging them from an upper tray in the author's Excalibur dehydrator

A view of the author's old American Harvester round dehydrator which he uses for smaller volume dehydrating.

Drying food can also be accomplished using the sun, but food dries best when the temperature is above 85 degrees Fahrenheit and the humidity is below 60%. If you live in the desert you might be able to use the sun for drying, but most places, especially here in the northeast, we often have a 80% to 90% humidity in the summer, so food would never dry.

There is a way to overcome this humidity issue, by using rising hot air, known as convection. A box is built with an angled piece of glass at the top. Mesh trays are spaced over one another at different levels in the box. Vents are placed in the bottom, and vents are placed in the top of the sides. The vents allow air movement, drawing air through the bottom vents and up over the food on mesh trays, and allows the warmer air and moisture to escape through the vents at the top.

This is a box type convection solar food dehydrator made by Mike Raubertas and used at his microfarm in Shepherdstown, West Virginia. Photo by Ruth Raubertas

This is an Appalachian Solar Dehydrator built by Cindy Conner at Homeplace Earth, LLC. Photo by Cindy Conner

A larger type of solar dehydrator that uses convection is called an "Appalachian Solar Dehydrator." This type of unit has an enclosed box to hold the food trays, but does not have glass on top of the box. Instead, a large collector is placed at an angle to the box, which has glass on it. Simply, this collector can be black on the inside to help collect the sun's heat, or even have some black metal mesh inside to further enhance the heat collection. This collector is placed at an angle whereby in is connected to the bottom of the box that holds the trays. The heat from the sun draws air in through vents at the bottom of the collector, and through convection, is drawn up through the tray box. It exits through vents at the top or top side of the tray box. The Appalachian Solar Dehydrator is more complex than a simple box type dehydrator, but it provides the most heat and least humidity for drying.

There are various designs for building your own solar dehydrator on the internet, and they vary from simple to elaborate. Essentially you are using the sun to dry your food instead of an electric dehydrator.

Canning

The canning of food in glass jars was invented by a Frenchman, Nicolas Appert, in 1809. It allowed you to preserve food by heating it in a sealed container.

Although canning is a great way to preserve food, I use this method only for those foods I cannot dehydrate, or preserve in another manner. It is time consuming, and if a mistake is made, your food can be contaminated with botulism which is potentially fatal. It also requires more equipment and supplies, such as jars and lids, which constantly need to be replaced. However, it is a good way for the self-reliant to preserve food for later use!

There are two methods to canning, and the method you use is determined by what you are canning. Depending on the acidity of a food you will use either a Boiling Water Canning process or a Pressure Canner. The intricacies involved are beyond the scope of this book and if you are interested in this method of preservation, I suggest you obtain a good manual that will provide you with the specific information needed to decide on the canning method. Two that I recommend are the **Complete Book of Home Preserving** edited by Judi Kingry and Lauren Devine, and **The Big Book of Preserving the Harvest** by Carol W. Costenbader.

A view of jars of canned hamburger. Photo by Jim Tompkins

If you use the Boiling Water Canning method, you don't need a special pot. If you already have a large deep pot that will accommodate canning jars and allow them to be completely immersed in water - the pot should be about three inches deeper than the height of the jars - leaving additional height for rapid boiling water. You need some type of a rack or spacer in the bottom of the pot to keep the jars away from the direct heat and allow the entire jar to be heated by the boiling water. There are racks designed specifically for this purpose, which allows you to safely lift the hot jars out of the pot. We use a steamer rack and have a jar lifter, that my mother used sixty years ago, that lifts one hot jar at a time. You could also use a round cake cooling rack that fits into the bottom of the pot.

But, if you are going to can low acid foods, you will need a pressure canner, which is a large heavy pot with a lid that can be locked in place and must have a pressure-regulating device. You don't want one of these things blowing up.

I highly recommend that you buy a quality Pressure Canner. My wife and I use an "All American" Model 915 15.5 Quart Heavy Cast Aluminum Pressure Canner with a metal-to-metal seal. It is made in the U.S.A.

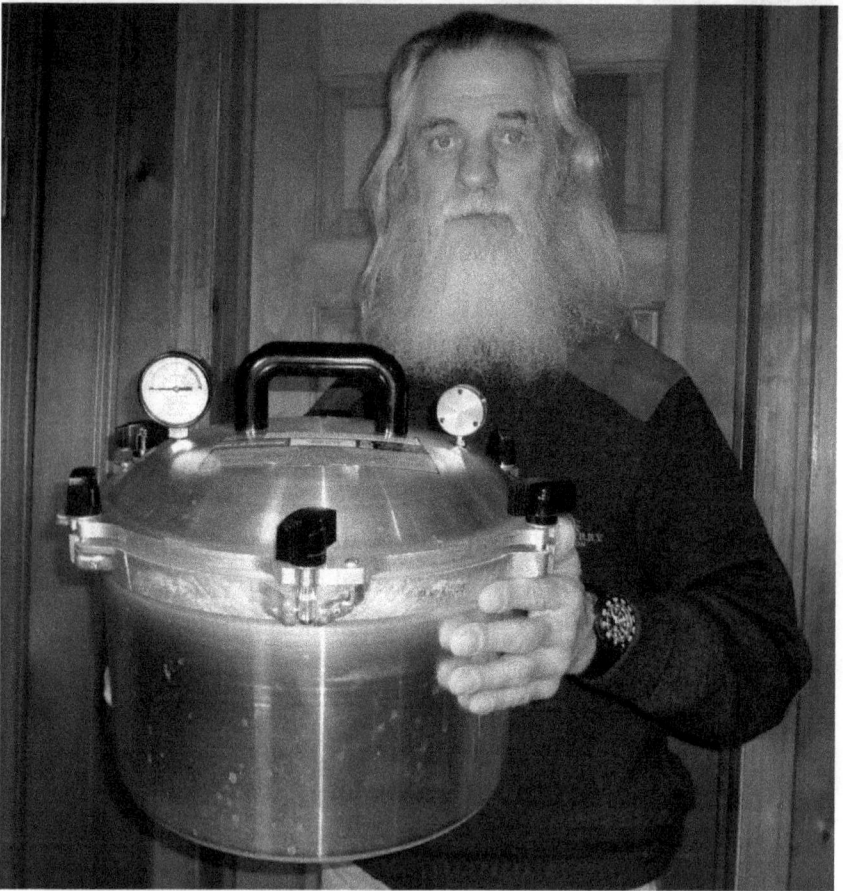

The author showing the size of his 15.5 Quart All American pressure canner. Photo by Denise McCann

Pickling

Pickling is an ancient technique of preserving food as well as an international one. Our ancestors have explored ways to pickle food for thousands of years.

Basically, pickling is a process of preserving food by anaerobic fermentation in vinegar or a brine. The first method is using vinegar which is a strong acid which few bacteria can survive. Most of the bottled kosher cucumber pickles that you find in a grocery store are processed in vinegar. The second method includes pickles that have been soaked in a salt brine to encourage fermentation. Examples of fermented pickles would be cucumber dill pickles and kimchi.

Homemade pickles ready for the pantry. Photo by Jim Tompkins

Of course, pickling is a little more than this and I suggest you get a good reference guide. The National Center for Home Food Preservation cautions that "The level of acidity in a pickled product is as important to its safety as it is to taste and texture. Do not alter vinegar, food, or water proportions in a recipe or use a vinegar with unknown acidity. Use only recipes with tested proportions and ingredients. There must be a minimum, uniform level of acid throughout the mixed product to prevent the growth of botulinum bacteria."

I'm not trying to indicate that pickling is difficult, and I make refrigerator pickles all the time. But you need to have a guide to do so safely. There are many books out there, and one that I have used is **Pickles & Relishes** by Andrea Chesman Pickling is another way for the self-reliant person to preserve some of that harvest.

Freezing

Freezing is often viewed as the most convenient method of food preservation, but the problem is freezers also need a constant source of electric power, which also makes it an expensive means of preservation. If you have a power outage, or even a mechanical failure, your food is vulnerable to being spoiled.

An advantage of a freezer is you can freeze most anything (there are a few exception) and you can cook large portions and freeze the extras for later use. There are also some disadvantages. If you do prepare extra portions of prepared foods, and freeze them, they have a relatively short storage life in the freezer compared to individual ingredients like frozen fruits, vegetables, and meat. You also need containers for the type of food you are freezing, such as plastic containers with lids. For fish and meat you will need freezer paper, freezer zip-closure bags, or vacuum seal bags.

If you use a freezer, it should be kept at a temperature of zero degrees Fahrenheit or below. I recommend keeping a thermometer, made for that purpose, inside your freezer which will show you the optimum temperature range which is between zero degrees and twenty below zero degrees Fahrenheit. Food can also get freezer burn, which makes it look discolored and parched, and there are dry spots on the meat tissue. This can be caused because it has been in the freezer too long, the food was not wrapped adequately which allowed moisture to escape the package, or the temperature in the freezer went above zero degrees Fahrenheit.

If your freezer is sparsely used, again, you are wasting power. If you overload it, you will get warm and cold spots. It is handy for that extra food that you can't deal with immediately, or preserve in another manner, but as they say, "Don't put all your eggs in one basket.

Smoking

Smoking meat is a preservative method for red meat and fish. Its purpose is to make these protein-rich foods last longer than they would not being preserved.

There are two types of smoking methods; Cold Smoking and Hot Smoking. Only the Cold Smoking is an actual preservation method. Hot smoking is the method you often see using home type smokers, and is mainly for flavoring the food. This method only preserves by cooking the meat during the process, and is not a long term storage method. Hot smoked food should always be refrigerated.

The Cold Smoking of meat and fish as a means of preservation has been practiced for ages. It is believed that indigenous cultures may have used smoke during the drying of fish to keep flies away. However, it was discovered that the absorbed smoke actually acted as a preservative as the absorbed smoke has antibacterial properties.

Cold Smoking is mainly a process of dehydrating and flavoring the food, which were often soaked in, or injected with, salt and/or sugar brines, or seasonings. These also aided in dehydration and preservation of the meat or fish. It is my understanding, from a friend that is involved with this method, that government regulators discourage Cold Smoking primarily because too many people don't do it correctly. It is safe if done right, however, it is further my understanding that in countries where they eat a lot of smoked food, they have a high rate of stomach cancer.

Smoking meat and fish is demanding as you need to keep a low temperature over a long period, and at the same time, keep it smoking for hours. Wood, which must be soaked in water, is necessary for the smoke and to keep it from burning up too quickly.

I will admit I am not real familiar with either method of smoking for preservation and have never done either myself, but only provide it here as another option for preserving food.

Chapter 4
<u>Food Storage</u>

Food storage is another important aspect of self-reliance. The previous two chapters dealt with obtaining food and then preserving it, but now it must be stored so that we can rely on these provisions, as if they were our own little grocery store.

First, let me state that I am not discussing long term food storage, such as discussed in prepping. My wife and I store a lot of food as we believe in being able to provide for ourselves in the event that something occurred that prevented us from being able to go shopping. This does not have to be a catastrophic event. People lose their jobs every day, and in today's economy, it may be awhile before a new job can be found. Wouldn't it be comforting to know that you have enough food at hand for a couple of weeks or months?

Lastly, I am a firm believer in using what you have. We do not store food for five, ten, or fifteen years. We use the constant rotation method. We always buy more than we need and we store the extra. We use the food we buy on a daily basis, by using the oldest first, and the newer food going to the back of the line, in the pantry. I will explain this further under the "Pantry" heading.

Jars

Glass jars are an ideal way to store small amounts of food, such as sugar, salt, spices, or food that you have dehydrated. You can save jars from purchased food like pickles, etc, which have a good sealing lid. Wash them out well and save them for storing your dried goods.

I like to use canning jars and vacuum seal them, especially for our dehydrated herbs, which we prepare enough of for the season. Of course, this method is not for wet foods which must be properly canned, but for those dry goods that you would like to extend the life of.

Some of your vacuum sealers, such as the FoodSaver, have an attachment whereby you can use a small hose attached to the machine and to a special mason jar sealer adapter that fits over a mason jar. This will allow you to use the sealer machine to vacuum seal a lid in place. There is also an item called a Portable FreshSaver vacuum sealer, that is a small handheld unit that can vacuum seal a lid, but you will still need the FoodSaver mason jar sealer adapter.

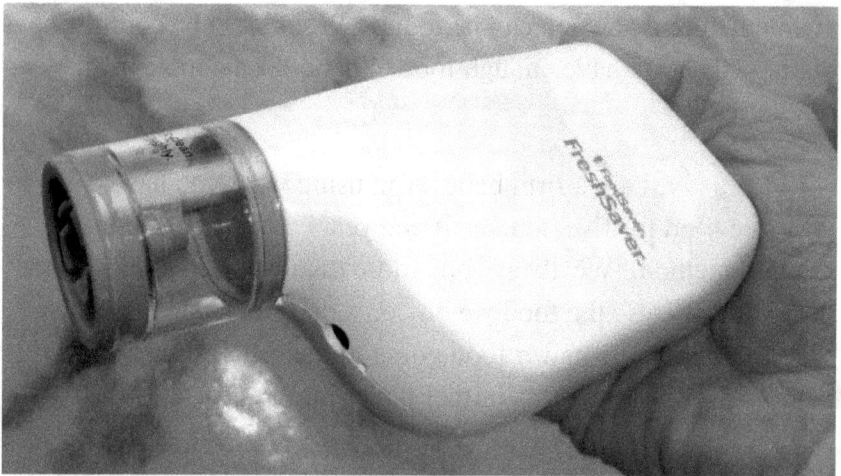

Portable FreshSaver vacuum sealer shown in author's hand.

Being self-reliant, I am always concerned with being able to continue doing various routine tasks even if the power goes out. The above two methods rely on electricity and, as always, I wanted an option. My friend, Jim Tomkins, is always searching the internet for new ideas and found a great way to vacuum seal jars without using an electric vacuum sealer on a site called

"Instructables.com". We both had to try it and it works great! Let me explain how it works.

The first thing you will need are the FoodSaver mason jar Sealer Adapters, which are available for both regular and wide mouth jars. If you don't have a FoodSaver machine, or if it did not come with the sealer adapters, they can be purchased separately.

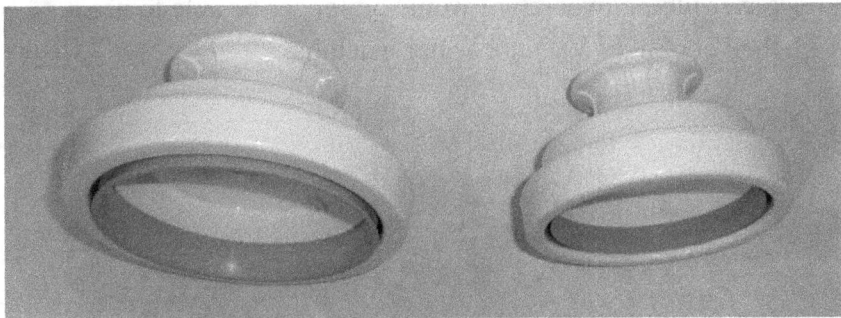

The above photo shows both the wide mouth and regular mouth FoodSaver mason jar sealer adapter.

The next thing you have to purchase is the Pittsburg Brake Bleeder and Vacuum Pump Kit. Yes you read that correctly, just stick with me a minute and you will understand. These can be purchased on the internet or at your local Harbor Freight store, and cost about $26.95. It comes with a lot of different attachments for bleeding brakes, but essentially you will only need the Vacuum Pump and the hose. According to the original internet article, they indicated you could use the conical tip that comes with the Brake Bleeder for use on the Mason Jar Sealer Adapters. However, I found this did not work so great as you can't get a good tight seal on the sealer adapter. Therefore a quick modification was in order.

The tubing that comes with the Brake Bleeder Vacuum Pump is sized to fit on the Vacuum Pump, but not the tube attachment for the Mason Jar Sealer Adapter, which is smaller in size. I took a short piece of aquarium tubing, which is the same size as the tubing on the FoodSaver, and using a tubing connector that came with the Brake Bleeder Vacuum Pump, I heated the end of the tubing with a Bic lighter, and forced it on one end of the connector. I then pushed the tubing from the vacuum pump on the other end. This allowed me to connect the vacuum pump to the tubing adapter that came with the FoodSaver for the Mason Jar Sealer Adapters. This also kept me from cutting the original FoodSaver tubing, whereby I would no longer be able to use it with the FoodSaver Vacuum sealer machine.

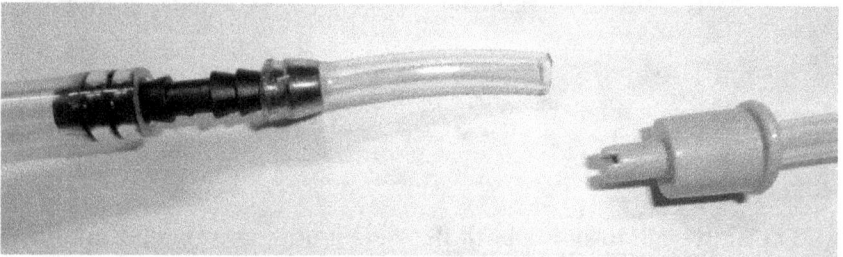

The above photo shows the reducer made to adapt the brake bleeder tubing to a smaller tube to accommodate the FoodSaver.

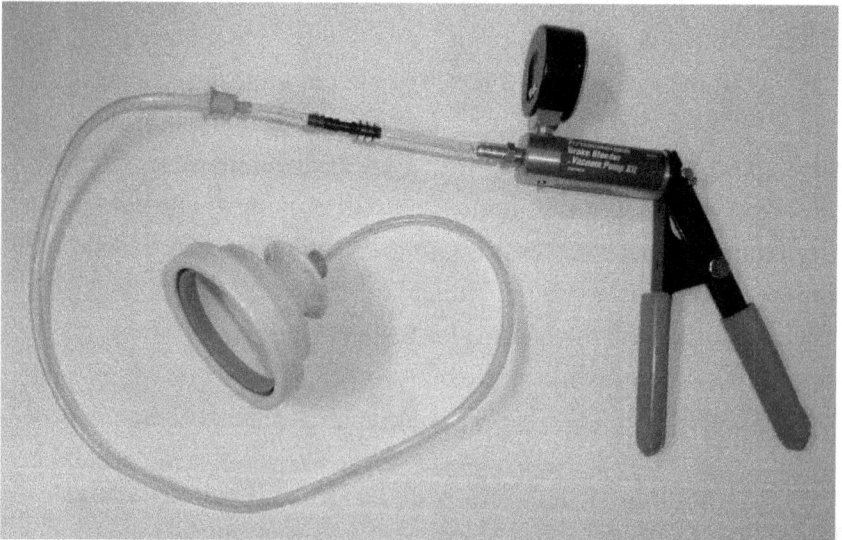

This is a view of the Brake Bleeder Vacuum Pump adapted to the hose for the FoodSaver mason jar adapter.

You are now ready to vacuum seal a lid to a clean mason jar. Just place a lid on the jar and then place the appropriate sized FoodSaver Mason Jar Sealer Adapter over the lid, making sure it is evenly seated on the jar top. Now connect the FoodSaver tubing to the sealer adapter as you would normally; it just plugs into the top.

Pumping the brake bleeder to vacuum seal the mason jar lid.

Now all you have to do is pump the brake bleeder until you have at least 20 inHg (which is a unit of measure for pressure). The higher the reading, the higher the vacuum. When you have a good vacuum on the jar lid, quickly remove the FoodSaver tubing from the jar sealer adapter, and if you did everything right, the jar is now vacuum sealed. Remove the jar sealer adapter.

Let me state once again, that you should not use this process as a substitute for the proper canning or preserving of food. Keep in mind that any food that would spoil if left out of a refrigerator will still do so even if vacuum sealed. That is why I use this for dry items such a dried herbs, sugar, etc.

Vacuum Sealing

Although we just discussed a way to vacuum seal jars, I would like to discuss the vacuum sealing of bags, which is especially useful for storing food in the freezer. As I've previously indicated, we dehydrate a lot of our food as I don't like to rely on a freezer in the event of a power failure. But we do freeze meat, and on occasion large batches of pasta sauce, or leftovers.

If you have freezer zip closure bags, and don't have a vacuum sealer, you can place your food in the bag and place a straw in one side. Don't place the straw on the food, especially if it is juicy, as you will be sucking on the straw and you don't want to suck the juice into the straw. For meat, you can place it on a folded piece of paper towel and stick the straw between the paper towel and the bag. You then zip the bag over to the straw, squeezing the bag tight against the straw. Then place your mouth on the straw and suck the air out of the bag using the straw. When the bag draws up around the food, quickly pull the straw out and complete the zip seal. Of course this will not be as vacuum sealed as when an actual vacuum sealer is used, but it will make the bag smaller, saving you room in the freezer.

If you do have a regular vacuum sealer, it is great for meat, especially if you have been able to buy extra that was on sale, or you have just butchered meat from a hunt. I recommend the extra expense for the heavy duty vacuum seal bags, and we get them on a roll, whereby you cut the length to the size of the object you are freezing. Again, a freezer is not my favorite means of storing food, as it relies too heavily on power to run.

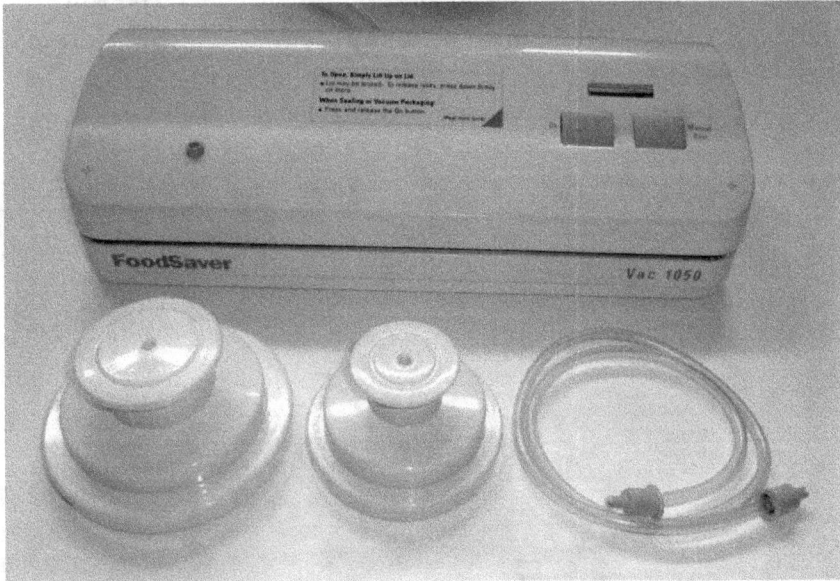

This is a FoodSaver vacuum sealer the author has had for years and that works well for the occasional sealing. The mason jar sealer adapters and hose are shown in front.

Mylar Bags

As previously stated, we do not store food for a long duration, but we do try to preserve our food through the winter. Another way we store extra dried food, especially our herbs, is in Mylar bags. A Mylar bag is a vapor barrier bag that blocks oxygen, moisture and light, the three big enemies of food storage. Think of a Mylar bag as a flexible metal can. However, because they are flexible, they are also prone to getting holes in them if you are not careful, which is why many people place the sealed bags in another container like a food grade bucket (these will be discussed next). I have found that for our extra dried herbs being saved through the winter, the Mylar bags are fine as long as you are careful with them and don't bang them around, or puncture them

The smaller bags, one quart size measuring 6" x 10", that we use have a zip closure on them so we use these for storing the extra dried herbs as we can take out what we need then re-seal them. However, if you are going to use them for a longer storage time, then I would include an oxygen absorber and seal the top of the bag with a heat crimp sealer.

This is a one quart zip-closure Mylar bag used for storing dried foods such as dehydrated vegetables and herbs.

A hand held crimp sealer is great for sealing Mylar bags as well as poly bags, and foils, up to 12 mil. thickness. It features a Temperature controller, On / Off indicator light, and is Lightweight and easy to grip. The jaws provide a 6" x 15mm with a Vertical line embossed seal. This is a real handy sealer for those Mylar Food Storage Bags.

For those who don't want to bother with a real hand held crimp sealer, which are relatively expensive, a flat iron can be used to heat seal the bag. Being this is not a study on long-term storage, if you are interested, there are dozens of internet sites and videos that show how this is done.

The larger, bucket sized, Mylar bags, which measure 20" x 30", must be sealed using a heat source, as they do not have a zip-closure on them. Again you should include an oxygen absorber which absorb oxygen and effectively reduces the aerobic environment to 0% oxygen. Therefore aerobic bacteria and fungi are unable to grow in this environment. This will extend the shelf life of a food product drastically. But again, this is for the long-term storage, which we do not get involved with.

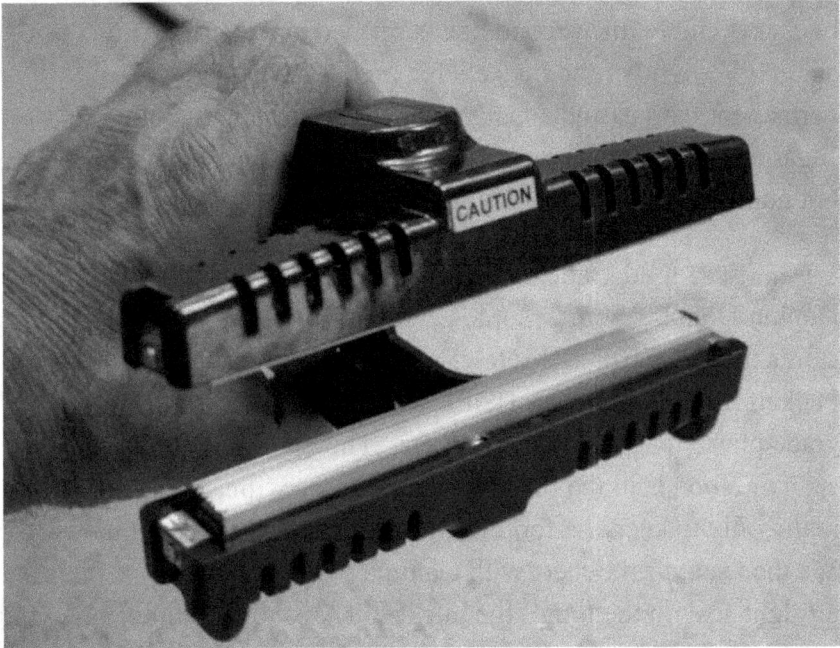

A view of the author's electric hand held crimp sealer.

Five Gallon Buckets

If you have the room, we have found that five gallon buckets are great for storing various dried foods, even though we rotate our food constantly. We store sugar, salt, legumes, rice, pasta, etc. in these buckets as we can buy in bulk, then use our buckets as if they were our own little store. Here is how we do it.

First, There has been some controversy on whether food needs to be stored in food grade buckets. Some say you need food grade, some say they only have to be HDPE with a #2 in a triangle, some say use Mylar bags with O2 packets inserted, etc. I think the bigger question is how are you using them? I hear a lot about storing food for 15 years. Again, I am more into rotating food as opposed to just storing it for the long term. Therefore, for food that we normally store, we use a minimum of 2 buckets. One is the bucket we are using, and the second is being stored. When the first bucket is empty, the second one is opened and the first one is filled again. We number the buckets for each type of food with a permanent marker and usually a label. So for a food item like sugar or rice, you may have two or more buckets of the same item, but numbered rice bucket #1, #2, etc.

I use food grade buckets only because I get them free from Dunkin Donuts. Some people get them from Wal-Mart, grocery stores that have bakeries, etc. I personally think even Home Depot buckets are fine (they are HDPE with the #2). I use a 3mil food grade plastic bag inside the buckets. These are fine for the time span the food is in the bucket, which I close with a twist-tie. It is really only to keep the food from direct contact with the bucket We then seal the buckets with Gamma Seal Lids, which provide an air tight seal on the top of the bucket. They work well because you can just screw off the lid, get what you want, then screw the lid back on!

Let's use rice, which we buy in the 11 lb. bags, as an example of how our system works,. In the kitchen, we keep our rice in a Tupperware container, in the cabinet. When it gets low, my wife or I go down to the Pantry and refill the container from the bucket being used. We take the twist-tie off the inner plastic bag, take out enough to fill our kitchen container, twist the plastic bag top and put the twist-tie back on. We then screw the Gamma Seal Lid back on and put the bucket back on the pantry shelf.

When the first bucket is empty, we start on bucket number two, and it is time to refill the empty one.

This is the Tupperware container that the author uses to store rice in the kitchen, which is refilled from a five gallon bucket.

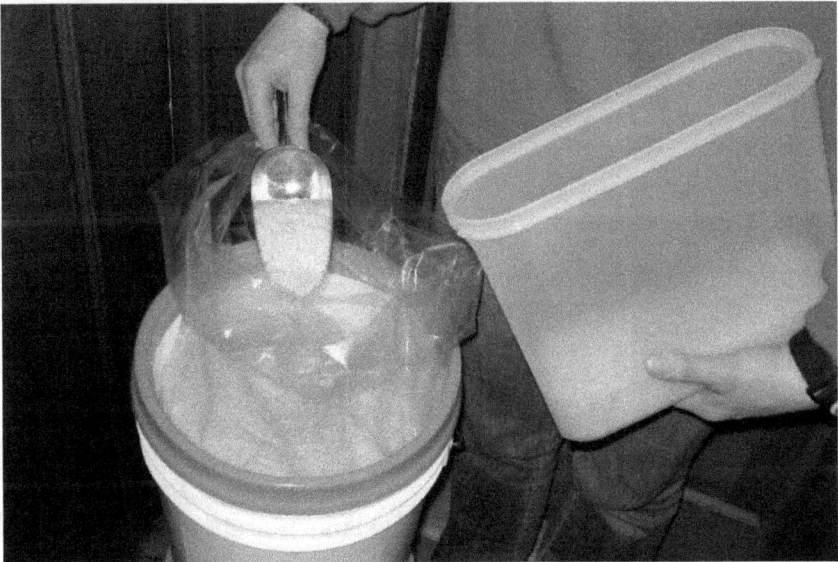

This shows the author's wife refilling the Tupperware container for the kitchen from the five gallon bucket.

The inner bag is resealed and the Gamma Seal Lid replaced.

Where To Store Food

Just because you don't have a large house, doesn't mean you can't store food. If you are creative, you can find places even if you live in a small apartment. You can store extra food under a bed. You can often find long plastic bins that have been designed for placing under a bed, and you can store food in that bin. When you need it, slide out the bin and grab what you need.

I have seen some people use an old trunk to store extra food, and it can double as a piece of furniture. A coffee table can be fashioned whereby the top hinges open and extra food can be stored inside. Look around your place and you might find room in a closet, or an unused corner, or space. You might be surprised where you can store an extra bag of rice or sugar.

Bookcases are often deeper than the books that are on them. Store cans and jars of food behind the books in that unused space. You can stack boxes of canned goods in a corner and drape a table cloth over it and you now have a new table for a lamp.

The important thing is to be creative Some people have unfinished areas of their house whereby the wall studs are open, such as the cellar. This area can be used by adding shelves between the studs and using it for jars and cans of food.

Look at cabinets that might have spare space, even if that space is on the top. Sometimes you can arrange jars or cans of food so they look like, well an arrangement.

When it comes to storing your food, keep a few things in mind. You do not want to store food in areas where there are extreme temperature changes. This would include the attic, which gets too hot, or an outside porch that might get too cold in the winter (if you live in a cold area). Also be conscious of rodents, or other pests that might find your food before you need it.

Having A Pantry

Not everybody has room for a full blown pantry, but your kitchen cabinets are your first line of defense for food storage. Keep them full and you should have enough room for adequate food for at least a few days. But as your space grows, you will want to have a dedicated pantry. Many of the older houses when I was younger had a small closet type room adjacent to the kitchen. It was lined with shelves and was indeed the "kitchen pantry." If you have the space, you might consider building one.

If you don't have the room next to the kitchen, there are other areas where a pantry could be constructed. I built one several years ago alongside the stairs leading to the cellar.

This is a view of a pantry the author built alongside the stairs leading to the cellar.

If you have a finished basement, or other area that has ample space then I suggest building a pantry as large as you can. You can never have too much room to store your food.

This is a view of a larger scale pantry that can hold a lot of food.

As you can see, pantries can be small, medium, or large. Utilize the space you have available and you should be able to have a pantry of some type. A pantry is your own little store for when you need food.

Root Cellars

In times gone by, before there was a grocery store in every small town, people needed a way to preserve their root vegetables and fruit through the winter months. Root cellars were the answer, and even though we don't hear much about them today, they are still a great way to store your harvest through the winter. When people think of root cellars they normally conjure up a vision of a big hole dug into the ground, or the side of a hill, covered with dirt. Of course this is still a viable means in which to construct a root cellar, but it can be simpler.

When people think of a root cellar, this is what they envision. This root cellar was dug by Steve and Susan Gregersen at their homestead in Montana. It is very effective for them, but a root cellar can be simpler. Photo by Steve Gregersen

I have heard of people burying an old freezer (the electrical part has been disconnected), door facing up, in the ground. A large piece of wood is placed over the door and then the top is insulated by various means. When you need to get into the freezer you just remove the insulation material and board. People have also placed a large garbage can in the ground, or a deep wooden box built for the purpose. Again the top is insulated. The bottom line is you want the food down below the frost line. Ideally, the temperature should remain between 32 and 40 degrees with a 80 - 90 percent humidity. However, this cannot always be accomplished. There are other considerations such as venting, etc.

Many root cellars today are built into the corner of a cellar, and this becomes rather complicated because of the variables involved. However, there are two really good books that will provide you with all the information you need about root cellars, if you are interested in constructing one. They are "Root Cellaring - Natural Cold Storage of Fruits & Vegetables", by Mike and Nancy Bubel, and "The Complete Root Cellar Book" by Steve Maxwell and Jennifer MacKenzie. I have them both and they are a treasure of information.

Chapter 5
COOKING OPTIONS

Before leaving the food part of this book, I thought I might identify some of the ways you can cook food that might assist in a self-reliant life style.

Of course, most people have a means to cook. A stove and an oven are normal accouterments to a home, but sometimes they won't work, especially if they are electric, and the power goes out.

I personally have a propane stove and the advantage is it provides me with the ability to cook even when there's no power. We have often had power outages and out neighbors know where to come to cook. However, a note in regard to propane stoves is that you should make sure that it can be lit with a match before you need to do so. Some of the newer stoves have a "glow bar" style ignition system that needs to sense current flow in order for a solenoid to open the gas valve, and you cannot light this type with a match. If you have a "spark type" ignition or "pilot light" system, then you can light it with a match. This is important to know if the electricity goes out. Also, most ovens also need electricity to operate, although not all. I advise you to find out the type you have before you plan on using it during a power failure.

Solar Cookers

Solar cookers are one of my favorite ways to cook as the energy used is the sun, and that is free. However, you must have the sun, and it does take longer to cook than by conventional means.

There are various types of solar cookers that can be constructed by yourself, or that are available for purchase. I have divided them into solar box cookers, which are enclosed, and solar cookers that are open. I use both types and I find the box type is better when it is cold out as they are insulated and retain the heat better. If it is cold, and the wind is blowing, the open type cooker is affected by heat loss mechanisms such as convection, conduction, and radiation of the heat.

This is a simple solar oven made by Eldon Martin from two cardboard boxes, one inside the other. Photo by Eldon Martin

One of the easiest types of solar cookers to build yourself is a box oven made from a cardboard box (see photo on preceding page). You basically use a cardboard box inside another box, with room to insulate between the two using crumpled up newspaper. The inside box is covered with aluminum foil. A piece of glass or an oven bag is placed over a large hole cut in the lid to allow the sun in. Another piece of cardboard is covered on one side with aluminum foil and is attached to the top of the outside box, so that it can be tilted to reflect the sun into the top of the box. I have built them, and they work, but are not as effective as other types of cookers.

My wife, Denise, and I wanted to build a substantial solar oven that would be effective and last for years. I had a piece of glass measuring 16 inches x 20 inches from an old picture frame. We felt this would be ideal for the top glass in a box type solar oven. We started with that and built a frame to hold it, using one inch square wood and 3/8 inch quarter round trim. It made a substantial lid.

We then designed an insulated box from 1/2" plywood and used Mylar material glued to the insulation for reflection on the inside. For the lid, we used another piece of 1/2" plywood with a piece of Plexiglas mirror, which was chosen so it wouldn't break. We insulated the bottom of the box and used a second plywood bottom painted with two coats of High Heat black paint, used for grills and wood stoves. A special arm was designed, that could be adjusted to hold the mirrored top at the correct angle to reflect the sun into the box. The results were very effective. For a complete article, and photo tutorial, on how we built this oven, check it out on our website at:
http://www.survivalresources.com/Articles/DIY_SolarOven.html.

This is the solar oven built by the author and his wife.

There is also the option of a solar cooker, which again is not enclosed. We purchased a commercial item called the "Hot Pot" solar cooker. The whole unit comes in a sturdy box with the reflector folded flat in the top of the box. The reflector is really unique and is made from a light metal material with a very shiny reflective material on the inside. It folds so the reflective material is protected when closed. The box, the "Hot Pot" came in, has a "box in a box" which holds a Pyrex glass bowl and lid with a black enameled insert.

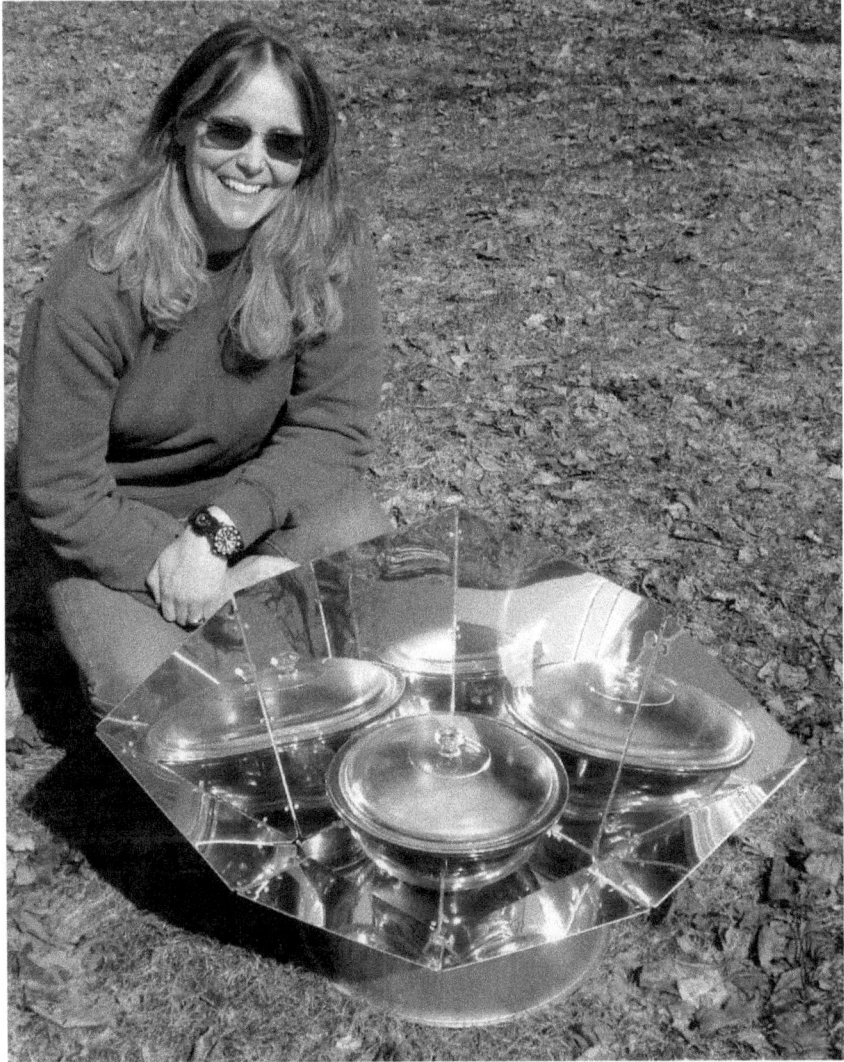

The author's wife, Denise, with the "Hot Pot" solar cooker.

This solar cooker is very easy to set-up. Simply open the reflector, which almost seems to spring open by itself, and set it down. You them place the black enameled insert in the Pyrex bowl and add the food you are going to cook. Place the bowl on the bottom of the reflector, add the lid, and let the sun do the work. We have cooked various types of food, as well as baked cake ,in the "Hot Pot" solar cooker with no problem. We liked this cooker so much we naturally ordered a second one. We now have "dual" solar cookers and can cook dinner in one while a cake is baking in the other. For a complete article and many more photos of the "Hot Pot" solar cooker, check our website at: www.survivalresources.com/Articles/Hot_Pot.html

Another commercial product available is called the SunRocket™, which is basically a solar water heater and thermos. You simply fill the thermos with water, open the panels and place it in the sun. If the sun is high, you can lean it back on the provided bracket, which doubles as a carry handle. If the sun is low, you can use it standing straight up. Although it doesn't boil water, it definitely makes it hot enough for making coffee or tea, and can be used for heating wash water when the power is out. It's made from an evacuated glass tube made from Vycor glass (95% silica, high temperature and thermal shock resistant). The aluminum reflective panels are made of high-quality scratch and weather-resistant plastics. It also includes a pressure relief valve.

The directions indicate that the SunRocket™ can be used to sterilize water, but in order to do so, you must ensure that the water temperature is above 150 degrees F (65 degrees C) for more than 20 minutes. The problem with this is there is no means for you to determine what the temperature of the water is in the thermos

There are a plethora of plans for building different types of solar cookers and ovens on the internet. Some are fairly easy to construct, and some get rather complicated, but everybody should be able to construct some type. Do a little research and you should be able to find something that will work for your needs and skills.

The left photo above shows the SunRocket solar water heater and thermos in the closed position. The right photo shows it open with the reflective panels open.

This shows the SunRocket leaned back on its handle for use when the sun is high. It can also be used standing up if the sun is low.

Butane/Propane Camp Stoves

A good backup for any household is some type of butane/propane/isobutane stove. These stove are usually made for camping purposes but are really handy if you have an electric stove and the power is out. I prefer them as they are safe to use in the house, as long as you have sufficient ventilation - crack a window - and are both economical and convenient to use.

A two burner Coleman type stove is handy to have as you can use it in the house or outside to cook when options are not available.

There are also many mini type camp stove that can fit easily in a kitchen drawer and be available when needed. I have several by Snow Peak and other manufacturers and they allow making a quick cup of coffee or a hot lunch a breeze.

Another type that is handy is called the Jetboil, which is actually a stove and pot combination. The stove and fuel canister stores in the pot when not in use. The bottom of the pot has a FluxRing that allows for very fast heating and is protected by a plastic cover when not in use. The pot holds 0.8 liters. The stove has a reliable push-button igniter and a stabilizer for the fuel canister to support the pot. The pot has a neoprene cover with a handhold so you can hold the pot when hot. This is a pretty reliable system for cooking small quantities. We have two, one for my wife and one for me, and they just sit in the cabinet in the event the need arises.

Various types of mini Butane/Propane stoves can come in handy for a quick meal in the house or out.

Propane Barbeque Grills

Something most people have is some type of propane grill for outdoor cooking. I have even seen these on balconies of apartments. They are a great way to cook when other options are not available. I prefer to have one that has the addition of a stove type burner attached to the side. The burner can be used by itself to cook in a pot and functions just like a stove in the kitchen. We keep several extra propane tanks in the garage in the backyard in the event that propane is not available, or we can't get out for awhile.

Charcoal Grills

Charcoal grills, of various sizes from large units to smaller hibachi type grills, are another option for cooking. Of course, you should have charcoal briquettes stored in the event that you need them. I know some people who store them in a 5 gallon bucket so they are available when needed.

One reason I like the smaller hibachi type grill is I can burn small pieces of wood in them in the event charcoal briquettes are not available, or you run out.

Wood Stoves

If you have a large enough kitchen you can have an old style wood stove. There are many modern versions and offer both burners and an oven. Some people have the best of both worlds, having a conventional stove and oven, and a wood burner stove. This is a future plan for my wife and me, but we just don't have the room at this point. Of course, you need to have wood available for cooking, so this type of arrangement would not be the best for a city type environment, unless you had access to wood.

For those small meals you can utilize one of the smaller folding type folding wood stoves made for camping. What I like about these is you only need small twigs to cook, as opposed to larger firewood. I have several different types that were purchased for camping and emergencies, and we find them as great options for cooking at home when need be. Even if you live in an apartment with a balcony, you could set one on a large concrete paving stone and cook. Make sure you check with management to determine if is legal to do so, in a non-emergency situation.

The above two stoves fold flat and burn small sticks. The left photo shows a Vargo Hexagon stove and the right photo shows an Emberlit stove. Both of these are ideal for cooking outside the back door for a quick meal and use very little fuel.

Fireplace

A fire fireplace is not only a handy alternative for heat (although not the most efficient), but is a good option for cooking. There are various types of fireplaces, and depending on the size, you have various options.

If you have a tall fireplace, which most people don't, you can hang pots from over the fire, like they did in years gone by. However, most of the fireplaces today are not very tall, but can still be used for cooking. You can place a grill in front of the fire and cook on the grill. This can be as simple as a small grill with legs set in front of the fireplace grate, or you can buy or make a special grill that hangs off the fireplace grate. Simple rake some coals under the grill and start cooking.

This is a unique grill that hangs off the front of the fireplace grate and allows you to grill food from in front of the fire.

Outdoor Fire

Lastly, if you have a yard of any size, there are many ways that you can safely cook with a wood fire. Make sure that an open fire is legal in your area.

If you have a small yard, or are not allowed to dig in the yard or destroy a patch of grass, there are various types of fire pits that can be set over the lawn, and are available commercially. Or if you're handy, you could build one yourself.

However, if you have the freedom to use your land as you see fit, there are many ways to build your own fire pit. It can be as simple as a ring of rocks or elaborate as you see fit. If you want to cook over the fire pit in a pot, you can erect a simple tripod to suspend the pot from.

A rocket stove is great for the self-reliant individual and is a very effective cooking stove using only small diameter wood as fuel, such as often found laying around a yard. Because of the chimney effect, the intense heat burns up the gases before they exit the chimney, working almost like a catalytic converter on a car.

One of my favorite, quickly made, Rocket Stoves is made from bricks. They don't have to mortared, just stacked together. I use a total of twenty-three bricks, with one of those broken in half, providing me with twenty-two full bricks and two half bricks. A piece of fireplace screen and a eighteen inch square paver and that's all you need.

You simply make a "U" shape with three full bricks and one half brick at the right rear corner. Over this you place the screen, and then do another layer with three full bricks and one half brick. You should alternate the half brick so on the second layer it is at the left front. You then start building layers of four full bricks alternating them so the next layer covers the spaces below that layer. There will be four layers of four full bricks and the completed stove should be six layers high, including the first two "U" shaped layers (see the accompanying photos which provide a better understanding of the stacking).

That is it and you can now fire it up. Using small sticks on the top of the screen, the fire will burn hot and be drawn up the chimney. You may occasionally use an additional brick to control the air entering the combustion chamber under the screen.

The above four photos show the beginning three layers of
a rocket stove made from brick, as described in the text
above. The finished stove has six layers.

A close-up view of the rocket stove combustion chamber. The
wood is placed above the screen and the flames are drawn up
the chimney. Air intake can be controlled by placing a brick in
front of the lower portion of the combustion chamber.

A view of the rocket stove cooking with a brick in front of the combustion chamber controlling the air intake.

There are many types of rocket stove designs and they can be made from various materials. There are various internet sites which show how to build different configurations.

PART 2
USEFUL PRACTICES & SKILLS

Chapter 6
RECYCLE & REPURPOSE

In this chapter we will examine different ways that you can recycle and repurpose various items that, in many cases, people just throw away. Oftentimes, people don't even think of other uses for refuse. I call this not being able to see the forest for the trees.

Old Newspapers

One item that I find very valuable for my needs are old newspapers. Although there are many uses for them, I find them very handy for two purposes. The first, I use an old cross-cut shredder that I have to shred them into small pieces. They can also be torn into small pieces but I find the shredder makes nice very small pieces.

This is a view of shredded newspaper for a compost pile which decomposes very well.

I save those shredded pieces in an old large plastic bin and use them in my compost pile as an additional layer of compost. The pieces decompose very well and I am returning something back to the earth and recycling something to enhance my garden at the same time.

I found an interesting product that allows you to recycle old newspaper into starter pots for seedlings or for young transplants. It is called the PotMaker® and is really easy to use.

As many of you know if you garden, in the early spring, you want to get your seedlings started and it takes a lot of small pots to do so. The little plastic pots that many use are not environmentally friendly. By using old newspaper, you have a very inexpensive means in which to make your seedling pots, and you help eliminate the need for the environmentally harmful plastic pots. What could be better for the self-reliant lifestyle?

What I also like about the pots made with old newspaper is, there's no need to take the seedlings out of the pot in order to plant them. You can simply place the entire pot in the ground and it decomposes.

A view of the "PotMaker" shown put together and the press and form individually.

The PotMaker® is very easy to use. You simply cut old newspaper into strips 3.5" wide by 10" or longer. You then roll the individual pieces of newspaper around the Press and fold them

under the end of the Press. You then place the Press into the
bottom Form, and press down.

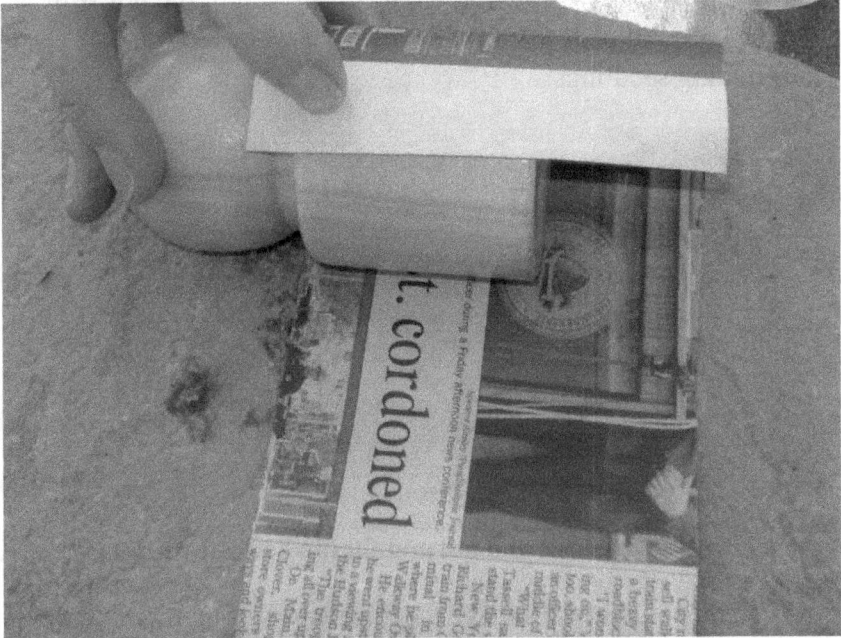

**Once you have cut your strips of newspaper, you simply roll
them around the press.**

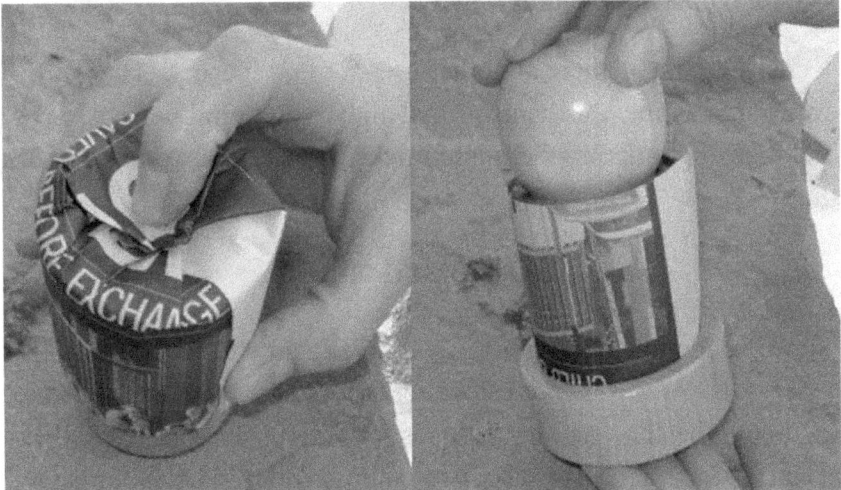

**Fold the newspaper sticking past the press over the bottom and
press into the bottom form.**

Once you have pressed the pot into the form, you carefully remove the press by twisting slightly, working it up and out. You now have a finished seedling pot ready for use. Fill the pot with some potting soil and sow your seeds directly, or use it for transplanting seedlings.

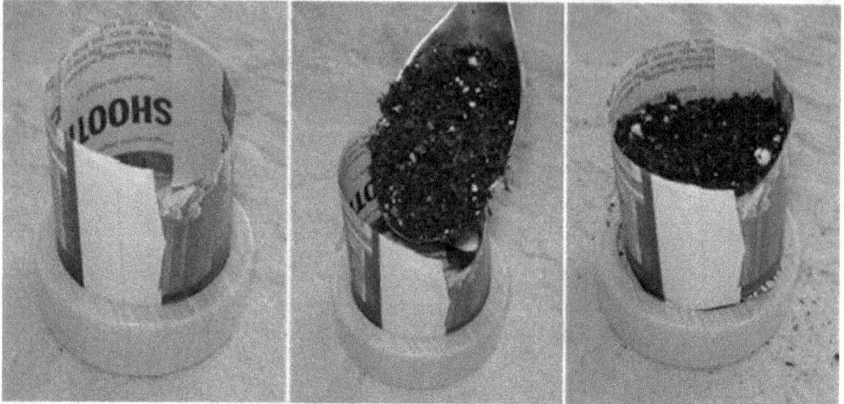

Twist the press up and out and fill the new pot with soil.

You could always make a device yourself that will do the same thing. A good friend of mine used a baby food jar for the press and another dish that the jar fit into as the form. It works great and cost him nothing!

Of course, there are other uses for newspapers. There are even some simple mechanisms that allow you to roll newspaper into logs, or compress them into bricks, for use in a wood stove or fireplace.

Cardboard tubes

Sometimes, something as simple as an old cardboard toilet paper or paper towel core can be repurposed for other uses. I have used both the short and longer ones for various purposes over the years. One of the best uses for the shorter toilet paper tubes is to organize the cords on various electric devices, or extension cords, when not in use. These cords can be folded back and forth and inserted into the old tubes in order to keep them from getting unruly when being stored. I do this with both appliances as well as power tools stored in my shop. As a hint from someone who does this, I normally wrap a layer of packing tape or duct tape around the tube when it will be used over and over again, so that it lasts longer with repeated use.

I have also used cardboard shipping tubes to store various longer items in the shop and they are great for take-down fishing poles. If you have a bow, these larger cardboard tubes are also great for making a quiver for arrows. Cover them with a little fabric, leather, or deer hide and add a shoulder strap and you have yourself a homemade quiver for carrying your arrows when out shooting your bow. I usually press a thick round piece of foam in the bottom of the tube so the points of the arrows don't push through the bottom

A cardboard tube from toilet paper being used as an organizer to store an extension cord. Notice it is wrapped with duct tape to preserve it for repeated use.

Old Wine Bottles

My wife, Denise, and I are always looking for ways to provide for ourselves. Whenever we can, we would rather make something instead of buying it. This not only saves money but provides us with a real sense of accomplishment. While looking through a catalog Denise saw a set of drinking glasses, and the catalog indicated they were made from old wine bottles. Drinking glasses are something that always seem to get broken so she said, "We should try doing this."

I had to design a jig to score the bottles with a glass cutter and devise a way to sand the rims underwater to avoid having glass particles in the air, which you should not breath. If you have an interest in making your own drinking glasses from wine bottles, I have an article on my website that provides a complete tutorial on how we made the jig, cut the bottles, and finished the edges. You can check it out under the "Self Reliant Living" articles section at www.SurvivalResources.com

These are various sized drinking glasses that were made from old wine bottles by the author and his wife.

After having made our drinking glasses from wine bottles, we had the tops of the bottles setting around for quite a while. Always wanting to recycle whatever we can, we knew eventually we would come up with a use for them. Then one day while playing with a new oil lamp that uses a Mason jar as the bottom, we wondered if the tops could be used as emergency globes for oil lamps. This would be especially useful in an emergency situation for use as replacement globes if some got broken.

We found that the many different lamps we had, used different sized globes.. But, using various sized bottles to make glasses, we were able to find some to fit those different sized lamps. Keep in mind, not all bottle tops will fit all oil lamps. If you want a top for a particular oil lamp, you might want to measure the diameter of the bottle before cutting it for a drinking glass.

This photo shows a cut wine bottle with both bottom and top, and three different oil lamps the author was able to use bottle tops as globes. The one on the left is actually a beer bottle top.

This is just one more example of repurposing items you have instead of throwing them away. As you become more self reliant, old things start to take on new meaning.

Old Clothes and Fabric

One of the things I often see thrown away, or placed in recycle bins, are old clothes. Old clothes can be used for rags; old t-shirts make great dust cloths and are great for cleaning windows. The material from old clothes can be used to repair other clothing, or to make new things with the material. When I was a child, my mother would save old jeans and cut them up to make patches for newer jeans. Today they sell patches for such purposes, but why not use what you have?

My wife tells how her grandmother would use old adult clothes, and downsize them to make clothes for the children. This obviously takes some skill in sewing, but having skills is part of being self-reliant.

One of the things we like to save is old pants legs. They are handy for making bags. My wife turns an old pant leg inside out and sews across the bottom of the leg. Then at the top, she rolls a small amount over and sews a hem in it providing a small channel. The pant leg is then turned right side out. We then put a piece of cordage through the channel at the top and this provides us with a drawstring for the bag.

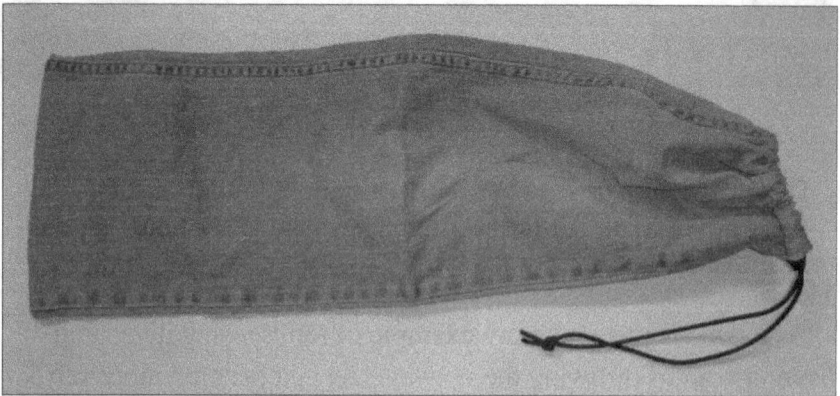

This is a drawstring bag that was made from an old pant leg.

Old clothes, bed sheets, draperies, and other types of fabric can be used for all kinds of purposes. My wife and I save all types of old material for use in making things we might later need. This material can also be torn or cut into strips and braided together. These braids can be used for everything from making pot holders to area rugs.

A handy item that can be easily made is a trivet using braids made from strips of old material Actually, the definition of a "trivet" indicates it is a metal stand with three small feet for holding a dish, and what we are discussing, in America, is often called a "hot pad" or "hot Plate." Whatever you want to call it, it is a device to place between a hot pot and your table to keep from burning the table." My wife is from Switzerland and over there they call them trivets and therefore we do as well.

In order to make a trivet, you need to cut strips from some old fabric; We often use old t-shirts, or other type material. These strips of material are then braided together and the braids are used to make the trivet.

There are two different techniques that can be used. The first is using three strips of material to make a braid. You then sew the completed braid together as you wind it around itself, making either a circular pattern, or an oval. The other technique, which we use, utilizes four individual strips of material for the braid. As you are forming the braid, one of each of the strips of material is used in rotation, forming both the trivet and the braid at the same time. This eliminates the need to sew the completed braid together to form the trivet. It sounds more difficult than it is, but too detailed to describe here. If you are interested we have a tutorial with details and photos under the "Self-Reliant Living" articles at www.SurvivalResources.com

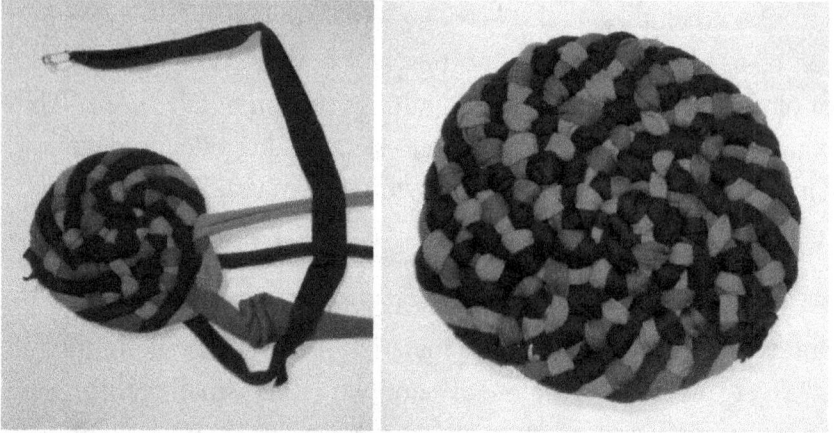

The photo on the left is a view of the initial braiding of a trivet using strips of old t-shirt material. The photo on the right shows a completed trivet that is eight inches in diameter.

Cans, Bottles & Jars

Old cans, bottles, and jars have many uses. Cans, especially coffee cans with plastic lids, and jars can be used to store all kinds of things in your home or shop. Cans are also useable to make small stoves and can be used as pots for cooking. As you become more self-reliant you will find many uses for them.

Old glass bottles can be used for anything from a vase for flowers to bottling your own flavored oils. You have already seen that they also make great drinking glasses when cut down. Old mason jars can be used for storing food that you have prepared (see chapter four), making homemade oil lamps, and a multitude of storage projects. The other advantage of mason jars is, you can get replacement lids, both metal and plastic.

Old plastic bottles also have many uses, and you are only limited by your imagination. I find that the larger soda bottles, the one and two liter bottles, are more substantial than smaller water bottles. Once cleaned, they can be used to store food, store water, and cut into various configurations. I have used them to make bee traps, bird feeders, small greenhouses, fish traps, and many other configurations.

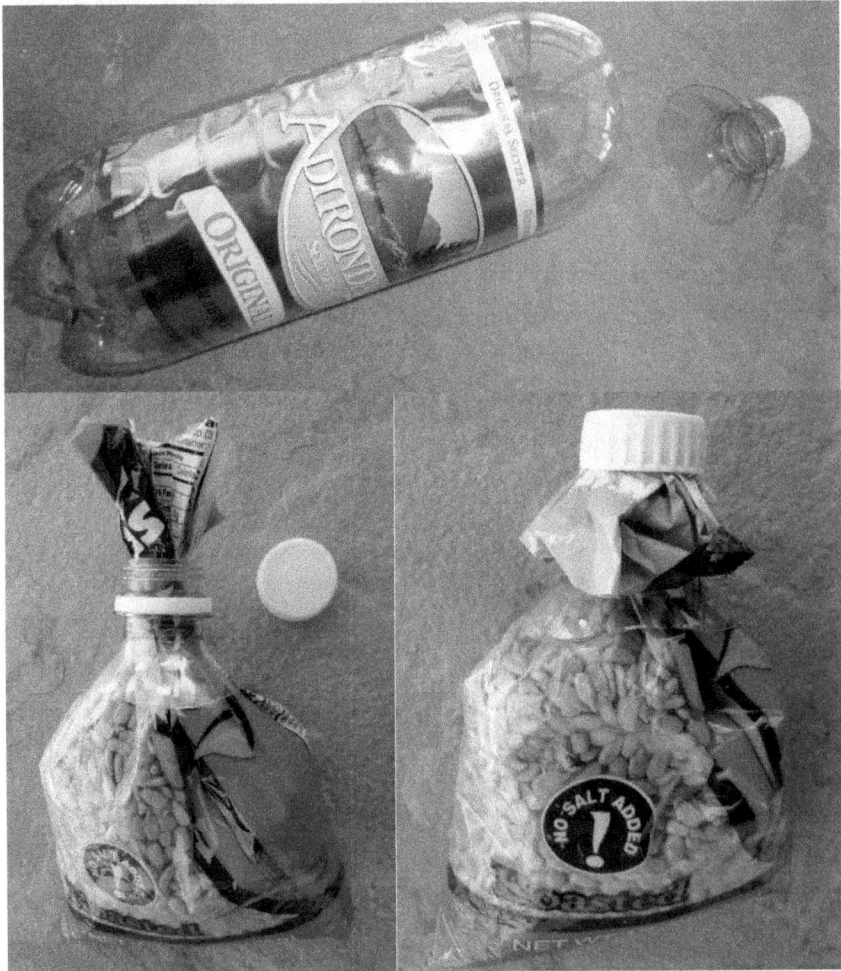

The top photo shows the top cut off a soda bottle. The photo on the left shows a bag pushed up through the soda bottle top. Photo on right shows the bag folded over the bottle top and the lid screwed back on.

Another great use is for reclosing bags of food in the kitchen to keep it fresh. I find this works great on partially used bags of legumes, sunflower seeds, chocolate chips, etc. First you cut off the top of the bottle, below the neck, leaving approximately one half of the outward taper. You then take your partially used bag, gather it together at the top, and push it up through the bottom of the bottle neck. When it comes up through the neck, you fold the sides of the bag down over the top of the neck, trying to keep the bag even all the way around. You then screw the bottle top back on the neck and you have a bag sealed for freshness.

Water & Milk jugs

Of course, old water and milk jugs can be used to store extra water, but they have many other uses. We have a bunch of old water jugs in our potting shed with the bottoms cut out. We set them over young plants in the garden in the spring and they act like small green houses and help protect the plants until they become stable.

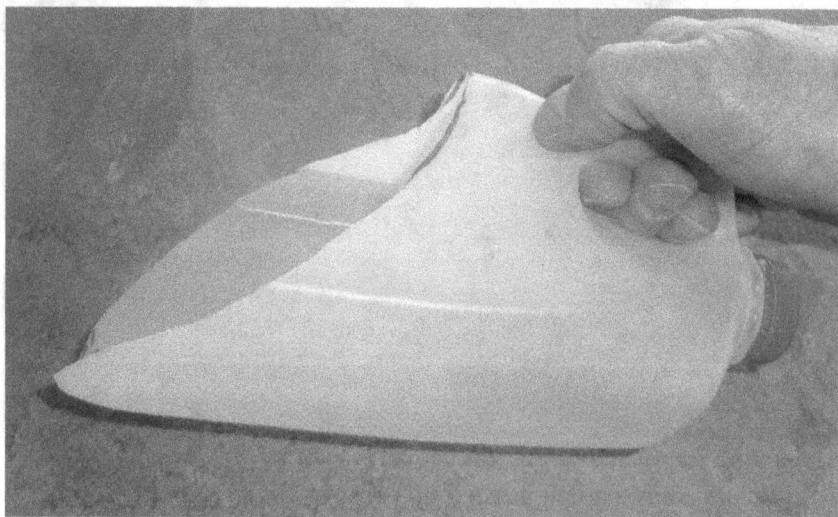

A scoop made from a half gallon milk jug. Great for use with bulk dried foods, grains, and animal feed.

These jugs can be cut up in various configurations for all types of use. One that I have been using for years is making scoops out of them. I find the half gallon size, being smaller than the gallon size, are a little sturdier for use as a scoop.

Miscellaneous Items

Even as a child my father always taught me to save old screws from anything taken apart. They would be stored in old glass jars or coffee cans. When you needed a screw you just went to your supply and found the size you needed, or as close as you could get. Even old nails were straightened and stored in cans. You would be surprised how many times I reused the same nails when building forts and tree houses.

The same thing applied to all types of hardware such as old hinges, hasps, drawer pulls, etc. Anything that could be used again was saved. When you wanted to build something you went to your supply of used hardware before you went to a hardware store. I still practice these lessons taught to me by my father.

Old wood is another item that can always be used again and again. If you have space, always keep your scraps when building something as they will come in handy for future projects. Sometimes you can get scraps of lumber at construction sites. Of course you should always ask permission before taking, but many sites just throw the scraps into a dumpster and have it hauled away, and will allow you to take it. Of course these scraps will be all different sizes and won't be like lumber that you can choose at a lumber yard, but then again it is free, and free is good.

Old pallets are another handy item for various uses and many businesses just throw them out. You can use them to store supplies on to keep them off the ground. They can be taken apart for the lumber, or even used whole. I have a good friend, Jim Tompkins, who used old pallets to build a makeshift structure for

cooking down maple sap for syrup. He also used them to build a structure that houses his blacksmith shop. All of the pallets he got free for the asking.

This shows a shed being attached to the back of a garage being built by the author's friend, Jim Tompkins, entirely from old pallets, except for the rafters. Photo by Jim Tompkins

Of course there are other types of items that you can use for future projects. I always save leftover screen, chicken wire, or other materials that can be used in the garden for building things.

This shows a very simple raised bed made from logs by Steve Gregersen in Montana. For the self-reliant, sometimes simple is best. Photo by Steve Gregersen

Raised beds for gardening can be built in various sizes and shapes, using diverse materials. They can be made from old boards, or even logs. They are handy for getting the garden bed higher than the ground, which makes it easier for you to tend the garden. Some friends of mine who homestead in Montana, Steve and Susan Gregersen, don't have an abundance of old wood, but plenty of tress. They often use logs to build things that they need.

Another area of recycling and repurposing is with electrical items. My father never threw away an old electric appliance without first cutting off the electrical cord, and I do the same today. They make great spares for when a cord on a good appliance frays, is eaten through by a pet, or is caught in a door. Just wire the old cord to the good appliance and it is useable again!

Being I dabble in electronics, I always strip electronic devices of components that I might be able to use for future projects. Items like voltage regulators (one of my favorites), resistors, capacitors, etc. A word of Caution in regard to capacitors. Depending on their size, they can shock or kill you, if they are Not Discharged before you remove them. If you don't know what they are, and don't know how to discharge them before removal, I recommend you leave electronic devices alone!

Of course, these are just some examples of various ways you can recycle and repurpose things that are often thrown away with little thought of the other uses they may hold. There are many more examples that could be provided. Hopefully, this chapter has given you some food for thought. Learn to think outside of the box and you will find many new uses for old items. As the saying goes, "One man's garbage is another man's treasure."

Chapter 7
Skills & Tools Of The Trade

I have always considered myself the proverbial "Jack of All Trades; Master of None." I believe in having the necessary skills to do those things, I need to do to be self-reliant, and have the tools necessary, to complete those tasks. This doesn't mean I can do everything or anything. But as needs present themselves, I endeavor to learn new skills that will allow me to be better equipped to accomplish the job at hand, without requiring the assistance of someone else.

Along with the knowledge, I also try to have the basic tools to go with those skills. I prefer manual tools when possible as they don't require power to use them. I am not saying I don't have tools that require power, but I try to back those up with manual tools, so I always have the ability to build or fix what I need.

I will provide various examples where skills and tools will go hand-in-hand in order to become more self-reliant. However, this is not all encompassing, and there are many other areas that can be taken into consideration. It should also be noted that this is not a how-to book. There are complete books written on various skills, and to try an teach all those skills here would be impractical. When you realize you need a skill, attempt to acquire the necessary knowledge to perform it, and the tools to accomplish the same.

Gardening

We have already discussed the importance of growing food in Chapter 2, and in order to do so successfully, you will need to obtain some skill in gardening. You don't have to become an expert, just knowledgeable in the various aspects of preparing the soil, planting, and harvesting. Of course there is more to it than that, but these are the basics and you must learn them.

In regard to tools, they are basic. If you are simply growing a garden in buckets on a balcony, the tools will be minimal, as a small hand trowel will probably suffice for your needs. But if your garden begins to grow to raised beds, or even a large garden in the yard, more tools will be required.

I believe that basic hand tools can accomplish most of the chores of a garden. As I have indicated, my wife comes from Switzerland, and she started gardening watching her grandmother. She loosens the soil in our garden bed with a simple garden fork The remainder of the chores are done with a rake, shovel, and hoe for weeding. We keep all the tools and equipment such as fencing material in a small potting shed that is back by our garden. This makes it convenient for working in the garden without having to run back and forth from the garage.

This is the author's potting shed that contains all the necessary tools and equipment for gardening.

These are the basic garden tools and equipment, used by the
author and his wife, hanging in the potting shed

This is the author's wife working at the potting bench.

Although the garden is loosened with a fork, there have been occasions when I needed to till some new ground for the first time. I didn't really need a big rototiller but, something small would be handy.

I found a small tiller made by Mantis that had a two -cycle engine and weighs only 20 pounds. It can be used by anybody and is easy to store when not in use. Not a necessary item, but one of those that comes in handy on occasion.

Keep in mind that a rototiller does depend on a mixture of gas and oil, so if you have a shortage of either, it will have to be replaced with manual tools and labor.

The author shows the lightweight rototiller made by Mantis.

Cooking & Food Processing

Cooking and processing food is a skill, and in order to perform that skill you need to have the proper tools. The skill of cooking can be learned by doing, studying, and research. I found that knowing someone who is good at cooking and is willing to teach you is best. I am fortunate, that even though I have always been able to get around a kitchen, my wife is very talented at both cooking, baking, and processing food. I did indicate earlier in the book that she was a home economics teacher in Switzerland.

I have found that an important aspect of having the tools is to have backups for anything that requires power. When the power is out, I want to be able to continue cooking or processing food. Many of your kitchen aids can be obtained as manual devices.

These are various manual kitchen aids that don't require power.

Even when it comes to my coffee, which I do enjoy, I like to have a manual coffee bean grinder. Coffee beans store much longer than ground coffee, which is good for food storage. When there is no power, I still want to be able to grind those beans.

I also like to have a couple of stainless steel coffee peculators that can be used on a stove, or over an open fire. These can often be found at camping supply stores. With ground coffee and a percolator to perk it in, all you need is water.

A view of the author's coffee grinder and two coffee percolators.

This shows some of the cast iron cookware owned by the author.

Most kitchens have pots and pans, but I recommend also having some cast iron cookware. These are great for cooking over a fire, and a good Dutch oven can be used for both cooking and baking. Although canners were discussed in Chapter 3, I again recommend that you have both a good water bath canner and a pressure canner, as well as a pair of tongs for lifting hot jars.

A water bath canner on the left and a pressure canner on the right. The front row shows an old pair of tongs for lifting hot jars.

If you grow or store grain, I highly recommend that you have a manual grain grinder. We have a well made unit called the GrainMaker which is made here in the U.S., in Montana. It can be manually operated by hand, and we also have an attachment that allows us to operate it pedaling a bicycle. We have a YouTube video on how to operate this grain mill as well as how to make "five-minute" bread with the flour you grind with it. If you are interested you can find it here:
http://www.youtube.com/watch?v=9XdxBGbcTNg and
http://www.youtube.com/watch?v=389x1Dv1kis

If you will be hunting, or processing meat for hamburger or sausage, I also suggest that you have a manual meat grinder.

This is the author's wife with their GrainMaker grain mill.

A manual meat grinder is handy to have. Photo by Susan Gregersen

This is only an example of the kinds of items that can make the job of cooking or processing food easier for the self-reliant.

General Repairs

Skills are important for the self-reliant and you should learn them before you need them. I have been amazed at how many people can't hammer a nail without bending it or use a screwdriver without messing up the screw head. As with all skills you must practice them before you need them, and utilize the correct tool for the job.

No matter the size of your home or apartment, you should have, at least, the tools to perform general repairs. This would include the tools to repair things around the house, such as minor woodworking and plumbing repair. These are tools that can be kept in a small toolbox that could be kept in a closet or garage, except maybe a saw, which could be hung up.

Although the tools I show in the accompanying photos are manual, it does not preclude you from using power tools, and I have many. But having manual tools to back up power tools allow you to make general repairs even when the power is out. These photos are also not all inclusive as I have many tools, and just wanted to show the basics.

If you get into auto repair, or more in depth repairs, I also highly recommend that you have a good set of wrenches as well as some socket sets. I have these sets in both American Standard and metric.

I also suggest that you have various screws and nails on hand, as well as items such as picture hangers, etc. You can purchase sets of these that come in plastic cases with dividers with various sizes of each. I don't have any to show, as I have many plastic drawers that hold all kinds of things I might need for repairs, as well as extra boxes of nails and screws. Of course if you don't have a shop, and minimal space, plastic cases will work.

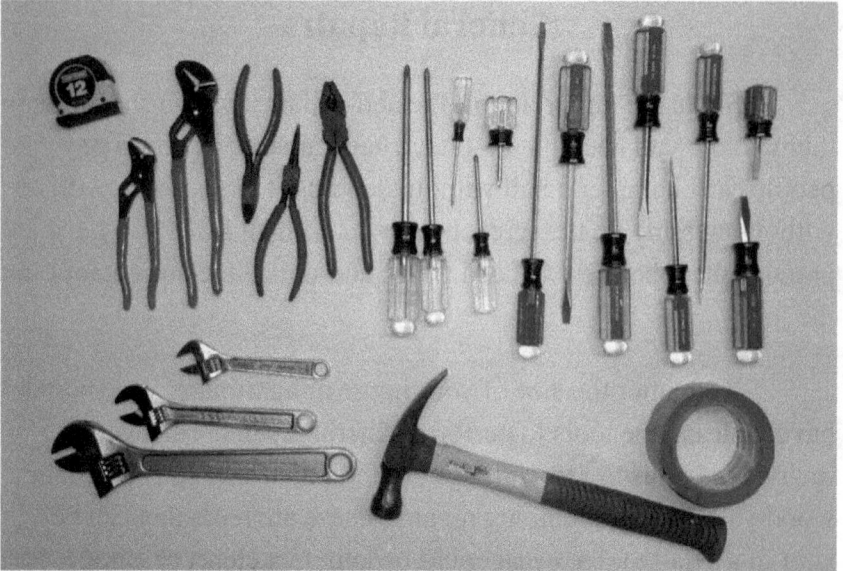

This photo shows some general repair tools such as a tape measure, pliers, screwdrivers, crescent wrenches, a claw hammer, and some duct tape.

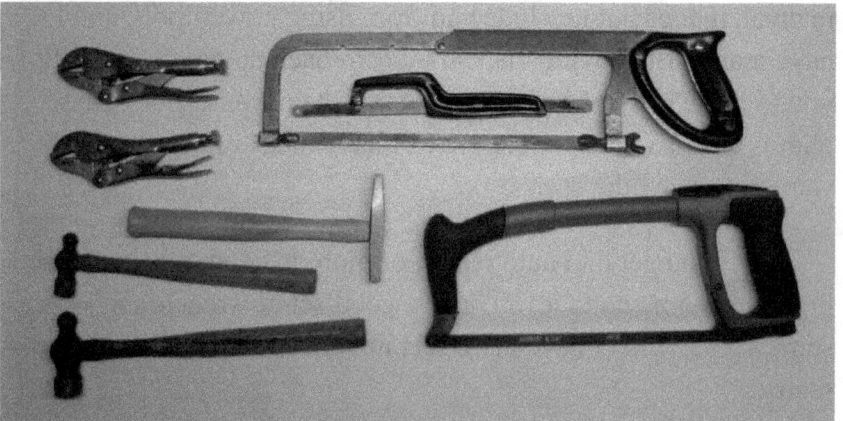

These are some additional general repair tools to include vice-grip pliers, hack saws, and some specialty hammers.

The more skills you have the more tools you will need. Basic woodworking and plumbing skills are essential to keep things around the house working, especially without hiring contractors to do it for you. Again, manual tools should always back-up power tools.

These are some basic manual woodworking tools. They include files, a manual drill and push screwdrivers, some squares, planes, chisels, and hand saws.

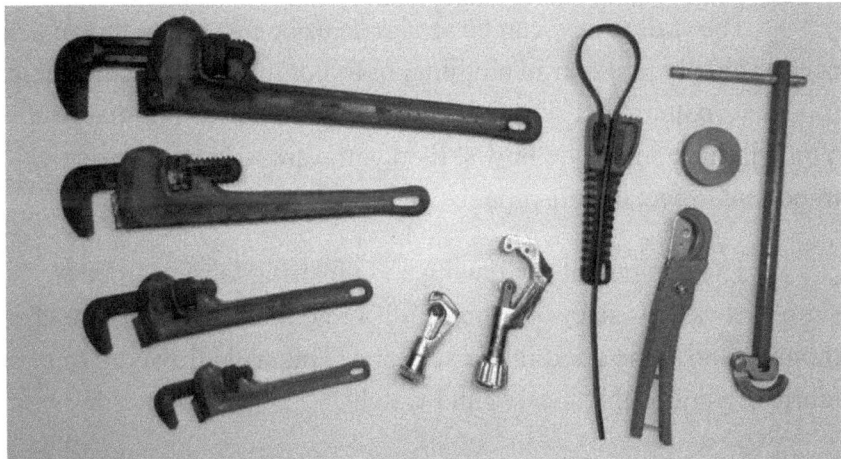

Some basic plumbing tools to include various size pipe wrenches, pipe cutters, a strap wrench, a hose cutter, Teflon tape, and a basin wrench.

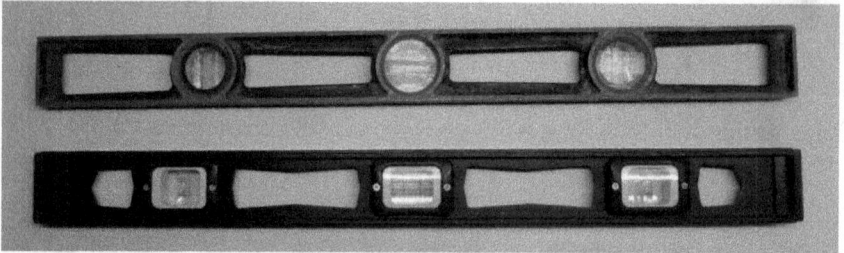

A good level will also come in handy when building or just trying to level a table or cabinet.

The important thing for self-reliant people, is to be able to fend for themselves when it comes to repairs. Learn as many skills as you can. We have only discussed general repairs, but there are many more skills that can be learned. Welding allows you to build things out of metal, auto repair and electronics requires a whole additional set of tools. You will see in Part 3 of this book, skills and tools will allow you to build water purification and alternate energy projects, construct heating and cooling devices, and more.

Sewing

The skill to sew can be as simple as being able to thread a needle and repair a tear in clothing, or as complicated as being able to make a pattern and sew your own clothes on a sewing machine. You will have to decide how skilled you want to be at this very important aspect of self-reliance.

The equipment for sewing and repairing fabric can be as simple as various sizes of needles, different thicknesses of thread, a thimble, and some good fabric scissors. This will allow you to sew fabric of various thicknesses and weight.

For thick material, instead of a needle and thread you might want to invest in a sewing awl which is inexpensive. I have also made a miniature sewing awl using a miniature screwdriver that holds different bits in a hollow back, with a screw cap. I use sewing machine needles, and store them in the back compartment.

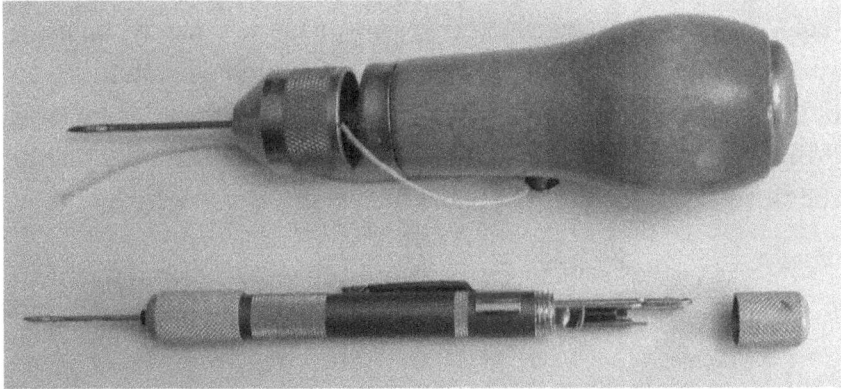

The top of the photo shows a commercial sewing awl and the bottom shows a smaller one made by the author using a miniature screwdriver, with bits and sewing machine needle, stored in the back.

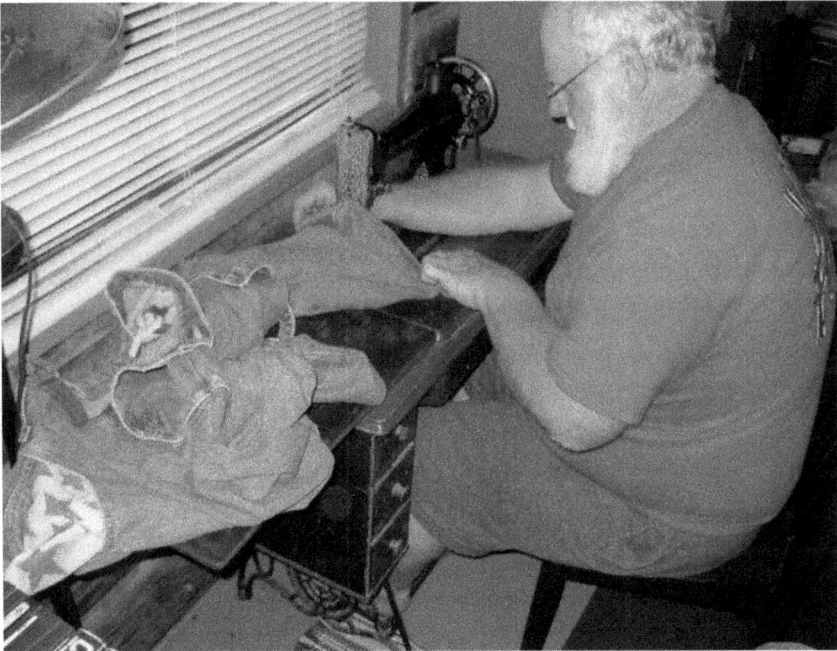

This is a photo of Steve Gregersen using a treadle sewing machine where the power comes from your foot. Photo by Susan Gregersen

If you are going to get serious about sewing then a sewing machine might be in order. There are some small hand-held units that I have not been impressed with, and are not recommended for real sewing. A full size electric sewing machine is handy, unless you don't have power. If you can find one, I highly recommend an old treadle machine that works on "foot" power. They can be difficult to locate, but they are out there. My wife had one when she was in Switzerland, and really misses it.

As well as sewing tools, try to keep extra material around for use to make or repair clothes. We discussed this under Chapter 6 - Recycle & Repurpose, and when something wears out, or is no longer used, roll or fold up the material and store it for later use.

Sewing supplies such as buttons, zippers, Velcro, needles, thread, etc. should be kept on hand for when they are needed.

For sewing supplies, they can all be stored in a small case that you can carry to your table or chair to make a repair. If you get really involved, you might want a larger caddy that can carry all of your tools and supplies. Back in the 50's my mother used to teach sewing at the Grange and Home Bureau and my father designed a caddy for her students. He would build the wooden frame, and then my mother's students would cover the frame with fabric. They would then sew the inside partitions, using cardboard between the material, so that the various sized sections could expand out holding various supplies. On the underside of the upper frame they would screw the lids from screw top bottles. The bottles could be filled with buttons and other items and unscrewed for use. On another shelf my dad inserted dowels for thread.

It is handy because when it is closed it can store nearly anywhere, such as in a closet or behind a chair. When you need your supplies, you hinge it open and it stands there by itself to become your sewing tool and supply caddy. I still have one of the originals and keep it as a memento of my parents.

The author showing the sewing caddy closed for storage.

This a view of the sewing caddy open with its internal storage areas for sewing supplies.

Making Things

As you have already noticed, this book is filled with various things that you can make, and there will certainly be more when we get to Part 3. But I wanted to present some specialty practices and skills. As you obtain more skills you will be more likely to make things yourself, as opposed to buying things. These are only examples and I'm sure you will come up with many more ideas as you become more self-reliant.

A skill that I learned years ago was the making of leather sheaths for knives and holsters for guns. It is a skill that allows me to provide for my own needs, and could also provide me with a bartering skill if the need arose. Nothing makes you feel better than having something that is useful and was made with your own two hands. I have a complete photo tutorial on my website at survivalresources.com for making both leather sheaths and holsters, under DIY - Do It Yourself articles. If you are interested in making your own, please check out the articles.

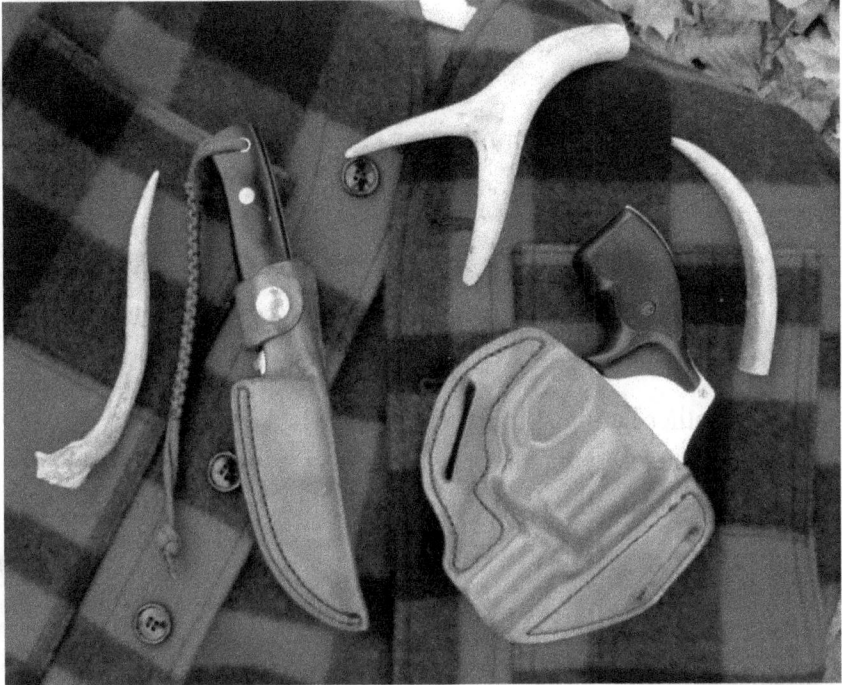

This shows a knife sheath and gun holster made by the author.

As with all skills, they will often require a special set of tools, and working with leather is no different. Fortunately the tools are few, but required for making a quality finished product.

At the minimum I suggest leather shears, a rawhide mallet, a stitching awl, a groover, edge beveller, sewing palm, harness needles, waxed thread, and leather cement. If you will be using snaps, you will also need those as well as a snap setter. Some metal clips for gluing and a burnisher. The above mentioned articles will explain how to use each of these tools.

This photo shows some tools the author uses to make leather sheaths and holsters.

Another handy skill is making bowls from gourds. This is interesting because you can grow your own gourds, then use them to make bowls, or other useful items like ladles, spoon holders, etc.

Top left shows a gourd from the garden, followed by two gourd bowls. Bottom shows a spoon holder and a ladle made from a tall gourd using part of the top.

My wife and I started doing this several years ago and have fun making things for the house from something you grow in your yard.

There are very few tools required to make gourd bowls. You can cut the gourd open with either a hack saw, or if you will be doing several, you can use a Dremel tool with a cut-off wheel. Once the gourd is cut in half, or in the configuration you want, you will need to clean out the inside and sand it clean. This can be done with various tools you can find around the house, but it will not be easy. I recommend buying a gourd scraper, for scraping out the rough stuff, and then a gourd cleaner for sanding. A gourd cleaner is basically a round sanding head on the end of a metal handle. These tools make the cleaning of the inside of a gourd a more pleasurable experience.

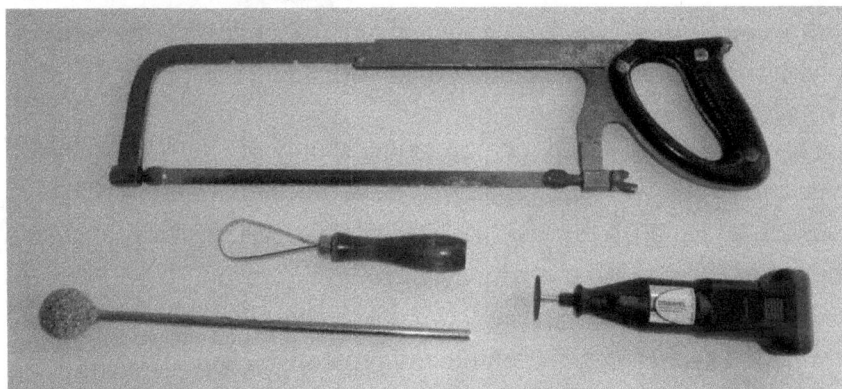

The above are tools used to make gourd bowls. At top is a hacksaw, below that a gourd scraper, and below that a gourd cleaner (sanding ball). On the right is a small Dremel Tool with a cut-off wheel.

The list of skills and tools for making things is endless. and a book could be written on just this subject. Candle Making will be discussed in Chapter 11 - Let There Be Light, and Soap Making will be discussed in Chapter 13 - Sanitation and Hygiene.

There are many skills for making things that would be useful for the self-reliant. Others might include knitting whereby you could make hats, gloves, socks, scarves, and sweaters. Spinning yarn, felting, weaving, blacksmithing, cobbling, tinsmithing, glass blowing, pottery making, wine and beer making, and welding are a few. Learn as many skills as you can and have the tools to accomplish the job.

Harvesting Wood

If you rely on a wood stove or furnace then you have your work cut out for you, no pun intended. You will need some serious wood harvesting tools and the skill to go along with it.

If you do need to learn this skill, and are new at it, an excellent book is called "The Greenhorn's Guide to Chainsaws and Firewood Cutting" by Steven Gregersen. He covers all the bases and it is available at Amazon.com in both Kindle and print.

If you only need the occasional supply of firewood, then you can get by with less tools, but the skill is still required if you wish to accomplish the task without injury. Even a small saw can bite you, and a small chainsaw can really injure you. If you are going to use a small chainsaw, even for a short duration, don't forget the safety gear. I recommend protective chaps, hearing protection, gloves, and safety glasses. You might also consider a hardhat with safety shield.

For felling trees you will need a good chainsaw or felling axe. For splitting wood, you will need a good splitting axe or splitting maul, and possibly some splitting wedges. For cutting small wood, which I often do, I find a good buck saw works well for my needs. I have a small, medium, and a large. The large was actually built by a friend of mine, Rod Garcia, who gifted it to my wife after she admired it.

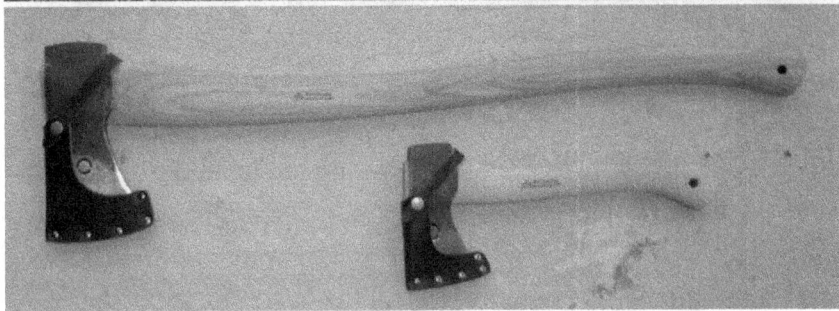

The top photo above shows the author's Stihl 16" chainsaw with protective chaps, hearing protection, safety glasses, and gloves. The lower photo shows the author's felling axe and a small hatchet for limbing.

Medical Considerations

The self-reliant lifestyle requires that you be able to handle many types of situations that might occur. One of those is medical situations. The first thing that everybody should be trained in is basic first aid, and CPR. You should be able to handle basic medical situations on your own, or at least be able to mitigate a situation until help can arrive, or you can get to a hospital.

If you are further from civilization, such as out in the country, you should obtain more advanced training. I also recommend, that if you plan on spending any time out in the woods, that you take a wilderness first aid course.

This basic training should allow you to handle many basic medical/first aid situations without requiring a trip to the hospital.

The next aspect of this equation is having the necessary tools and supplies to treat cuts, wounds, or other conditions. I will not go into a list of thing that you need, but you should keep in mind that you should choose supplies that you know how to use. I have seen a lot of people buy these large first aid kits and don't know how to use most of the stuff in them.

You should have a well equipped first aid kit, but I always recommend building it yourself with items you know how to use. It should be in some type of container so that it can be grabbed and taken to the problem, as opposed to taking the injured to the kit. I have our basic kit built in a large tackle box and it has its own shelf for storage in the hallway. Everyone knows where it is and can grab it at a moment's notice. It has all the basics for immediate needs. Of course we have much more in-depth and detailed equipment and supplies in a cabinet, but that is for larger problems.

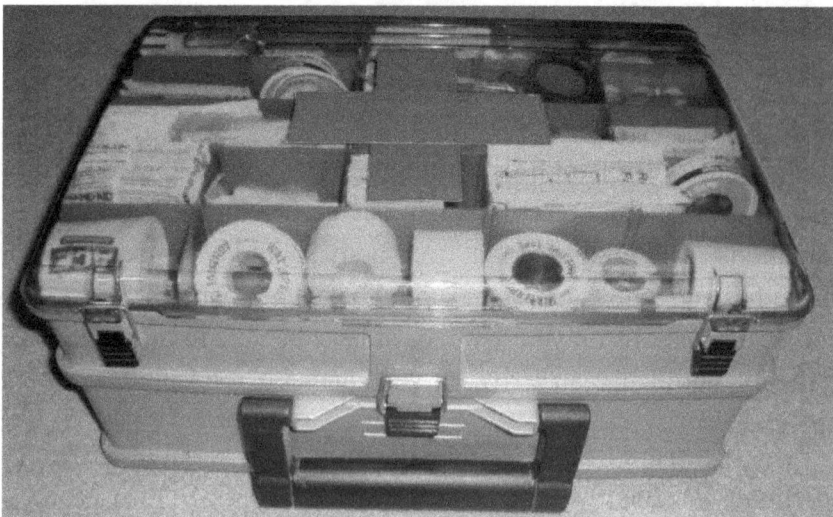

This is the author's basic first aid kit built into a large tackle box. It is kept handy in the hallway in the event it is needed quick.

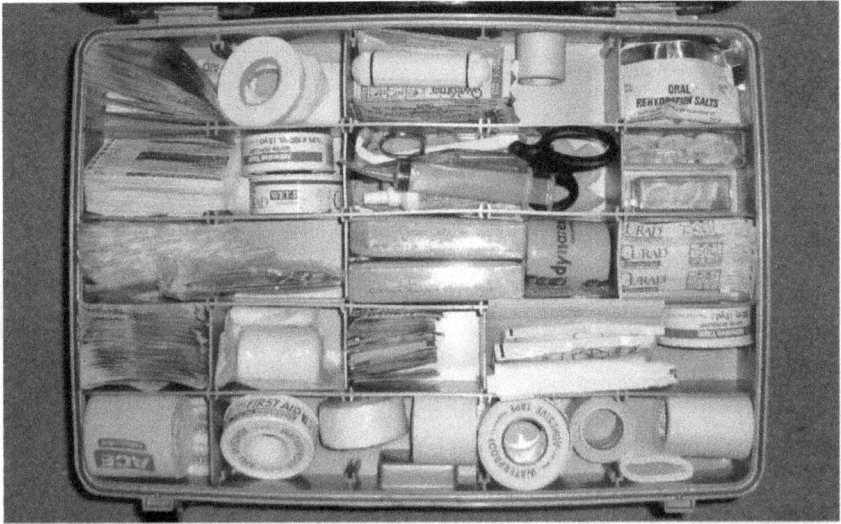

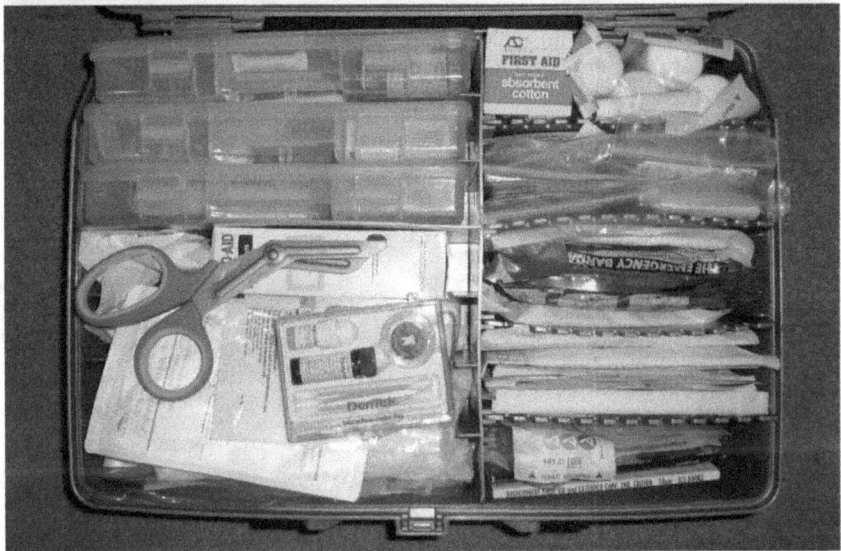

The top photo shows the inside top portion of the author's basic first aid kit, and the bottom shows the bottom portion.

You will see throughout this book that having skills, and the tools to use those skills, are an important aspect of self-reliance.

Chapter 8
<u>Just In Case Supplies</u>

As I indicated in the Introduction, this is not a book on emergency preparedness, per se. Even though we have discussed various skills that are germane to self-reliance, having adequate supplies in the event of an emergency or an unexpected situation is a prudent measure. The situation could be weather related, an unexpected situation affecting your area or the country, or simply you could become unemployed and need to exist for an unspecified amount of time without a paycheck.

Even though we will discuss different types of supplies you should keep on hand, it should be noted that some supplies should be kept separate from those in your home. We keep five gallon buckets in our potting shed which have extra clothes and foot wear, as well as emergency supplies, to include water purification. In the event we had a fire at the house, we would have the essentials to take care of our basic needs. If you don't have a place on your property, you could always use a storage rental to keep some basics.

Books

Although not an actual emergency supply, one thing I always like to have plenty of is how-to books. Although you should learn skills and practice them, nobody can remember everything. I probably have more books than most, but I have always been an avid collector. I often hear people say that they have a huge collection of how-to books on their Kindle, but in an emergency, especially without power to recharge your Kindle, a collection of hard copy books will be appreciated. I usually reserve my Kindle for novels.

We keep our books in various areas and segregate them by type of book, such as how-to, plant identification, cook books, self-reliant living, wilderness survival, etc. The majority are kept on a large book shelf in the living room, but some are kept in different areas for convenience. Our plant identification books in the dining room, cookbooks in the dinette, etc.

This shows some of the author's plant identification books which are kept on a separate bookshelf in the dining room.

This is a view of the author's large bookcase in the living room.

Miscellaneous Supplies

Paper goods are always a good supply item to have on hand. This would include toilet paper and paper towels. Paper goods would also include paper plates. We keep a five gallon bucket full of paper plates, as they fit in a bucket nicely. In a situation without water, paper plates are great for serving food. When you are done eating you can simply burn them. Although not paper, don't forget a few boxes of plastic utensils, as you won't have to wash them, saving water. They can be collected up after a meal and stored in a large plastic bag until they can be disposed of.

Another item, is various sizes of garbage bags and zip-closure bags. They are handy for all types of uses, from storing food to garbage. Contractor bags have uses to include using one as a poncho. Extra cleaning supplies are also handy.

This shows how you could store a supply of extra paper goods, garbage and zip-closure bags, shampoo, handy wipes, etc.

Plastic cutlery is very inexpensive and can be purchased in boxes of hundreds of units, yet take up very little space. Spoons are probably used more than forks.

We will be discussing lighting in Chapter 11, but if you use oil lamps, you should always keep spare lamp oil on hand. Nothing worse than needing your lamps, and you run out of fuel the first day.

If you will be depending on oil lamps when the power goes out, make sure you store some extra lamp oil.

One item I often see left out of extra supplies are extra matches or lighters. When the power is out, you will be lighting lamps, candles, stoves, and possibly making fires. Even though we will be discussing bartering in the next chapter, lighters and matches are a great barter item as everyone will need some if something major occurs.

Strike anywhere matches can be purchased in most hardware stores and are handy because you don't need the striker on the side of the box to light them. We buy the large size and vacuum seal them in long blocks of ten boxes, then store them in the pantry. We also buy the smaller boxes by the large package and store them as well. We like BIC lighters so we buy them a few at a time and store them in an old 7.62 ammo can.

Extra matches can be vacuum sealed and stored for later use.

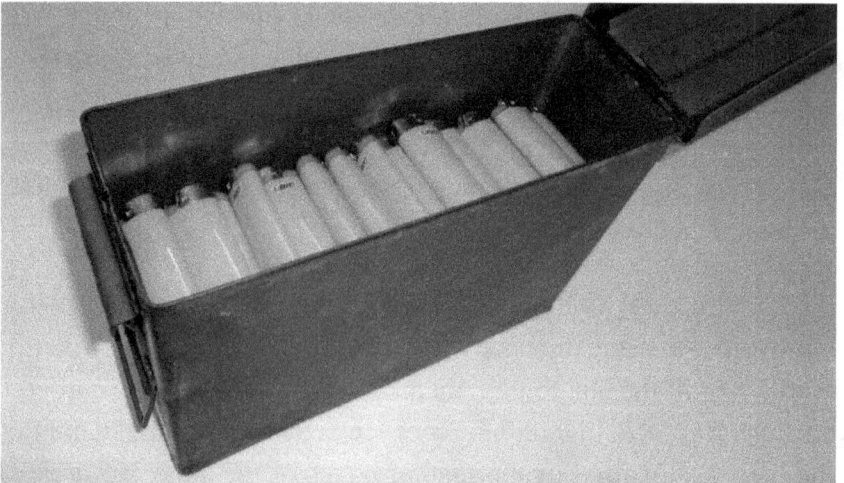

Large BIC lighters fit and store easily in an old 7.62 ammo can.

In Chapter 3 we discussed food preservation and if you plan on canning, it is always handy to have extra canning jars, and a lot of lids. Jars can be reused, but lids cannot, so store plenty of those.

If you plan on canning food, keep plenty of extra jars on hand.

Canning jars can be reused, but lids cannot. Store lots of extras.

Your immediate emergency supplies should be stored in a convenient location so that you can get to them quickly and easily. We store the basics just outside the cellar door in a shelving unit I built that precedes our small pantry. When we need something we can get to it and grab it without having to search around, or go digging. We also keep two headlamps hanging on the wall outside the door. If the power goes out at night, we can grab our headlamps first, which makes it much easier to see everything else.

Basic emergency supplies kept outside the cellar door alongside the small pantry

As you can see, if there are things that you do, or need, to be self-reliant, you should keep extra supplies that will allow you to continue doing those things, even if an incident occurs that might prevent you from going out and re-supplying. There are many more types of items that could be discussed, but I'm sure you get the idea. Don't be caught short on supplies when you need them most.

Chapter 9
<u>Don't Bank On Banks</u>

This may sound like a contradiction of terms, but let me explain. As we have discussed earlier, in order to be self-reliant you can't rely on others for everything. However, most people rely on banks for the holding, safekeeping and the dispersing of their money. Many people today don't even see their money on payday, but instead, have it deposited directly into their bank account. This is with the blind faith, that when they want it, it will be available.

In most cases the system works. But what if it didn't? What if the bank's closed and didn't open back up. I'm sure you are thinking that this is very unlikely to happen, but it could.

On March 6, 1933 President Franklin D. Roosevelt declared a "Bank Holiday" for four days in an attempt to prevent a run on banks. Of course that was a long time ago but on March 16, 2013, all banks in Cyprus closed for two weeks, in order to avert a run on deposits. When they reopened, they did so with strict restrictions on transactions, such as a limit on cash withdrawals, and no checks being cashed. The banks had planned on seizing ten percent of all bank accounts to help keep the government afloat, but that did not occur.

There are already limits in the U.S. on the amount of money you may withdraw from your own account without a report being filled out and sent to the government. On large withdrawals, some banks have actually asked people why they want the money, almost as if it was the banks money, and not yours.

Many people rely on their bills being paid through the bank. They trust that when they need their money, it will be available. After all, their money is insured by the government.

But that insurance, the FDIC (Federal Deposit Insurance Corporation) guarantees that every depositor will receive up to $250,000.00 of their deposits. Anything over this amount is not insured, and if our financial system collapsed, where would they get the money to pay everybody? They wouldn't, and you would be out the money.

Also keep in mind that we are not talking strictly banks here. We are talking ATM's and charge cards. They are all tied to the banking system. If banks fail, ATM's will fail, and your charge cards will fail. If charge cards fail, when you go into the grocery store to buy food, you will need cash. Have you ever played dominoes? Well then you get the idea.

If banks closed and ATM's and charge cards failed to work, how much cash do you have on hand to buy things?

Keep in mind that an occurrence like this does not require our monetary system to crash. This could also be a result of a crash of the power grid. It doesn't even have to be a major incident like an EMP (Electromagnetic Pulse). It could simply be a local power failure. I have gone ten days without power in our area and most of the grocery, and other stores, closed their doors.

The big question is how long could you go if something like this did happen? Days, weeks, months. I see people everyday buying coffee in the morning using charge cards. Do they have any cash on hand, or do they literally rely on the banking system for their very existence? If you want to be self-reliant, don't rely completely on banks.

Cash Is King

Everybody should have some cash on hand. When I was young, everybody had a least a few dollars in a coffee can. As we saw above, you can't rely on an ATM for any cash you need. I always recommend having at least a couple of hundred dollars secured at your home, if not more. It should not be kept in a coffee can, but in an area that is safe from theft and fire. Everybody should be able to afford a small "Sentry" type safe that can hold your cash and other small valuables. These types of fireproof safes are easily concealed in the home.

Keep in mind, that cash can also fail. It would take a complete collapse of our monetary system, but it could happen. Our money used to be backed by gold. However, in 1971 President Richard Nixon announced to the world that the U.S. dollar was no longer backed by gold, even though he still wanted the world to use the dollar as the "reserve currency."

The problem with the dollar today is inflation. And with the government pumping out new bills like Pez from a Pez dispenser, and a deficit growing every day, I don't see an end to inflation. I told my wife, who you now know is from Switzerland, that when I was young I used to pay twenty-five cents for a gallon of gas, and now I pay almost $4.00. I asked how the price of gas could increase 1,550 percent over forty-five years. She quickly said, "It didn't, inflation has reduced the worth of dollar by that much." Think about it; of course the price of things has increased in forty-five years, but the majority of the increase in price is a decrease in the worth of our dollar.

Until we can come up with something better, cash will still be king, at least as long as we are allowed to use it. There are rumors, but for now, if you want to be able to take care of your needs, keep some cash on hand.

Eliminating Debt

Freedom comes at a price, and a priority for anyone who wants to be self-reliant is eliminating debt. Nothing makes you more dependent on others than debt. When you owe other people you are indebted to them, and have an obligation to pay them back.

Reducing debt is not always easy, but it can be done. First you must return to the "Needs vs. Wants" axiom. This starts with having a budget. Unfortunately, you cannot function like our government does and spend more than you have coming in, because you don't have the luxury of being able to just print more money, or tax other people to make up for your overspending. Our government has a Seventeen Trillion dollar deficit because they have never learned this basic principal. You cannot spend more than you make, at least not for long.

Determine what your income is per month, and then determine what your actual expenses are per month. You must be honest here and include ALL expenses. If you have expenses that only occur every six months, or annually (like land tax, etc.) then those expenses must be amortized so that each month a portion of that expense is saved, or put away, for when the debt is due.

If your expenses per month are more than your income then you have some serious decisions to make. You will either need to reduce some of your expenses, or increase your income. You need to set up a budget that will allow you to pay your bills and have something left over for savings. This is a simplification, but the only real way to reduce debt. The more you make, and the less you spend on expenses, the more you will have for savings, and to pay down the debt you already have. There is no magic involved here. It is as simple as that.

Once you have determined a budget, you need to get your charge cards under control. I would say eliminate them, but they can come in handy at times. However, if you use them, then use them like cash. If you can't afford cash for your purchase, then you probably can't afford the charge. If you are buying a larger "Need" item like a new furnace or stove, and you can't wait, then you should have the extra money in your budget for that additional monthly payment. Keep in mind that if you do not pay off the purchase the first month, you will be paying interest which adds to the cost of each item.

I have found over the years that if you get your charge cards under control, and save money, you are less likely to need them. If I use a charge card now, the balance is always paid when the bill arrives.

The hardest debt to eliminate is a mortgage, but that too can be done. I know many people who have a huge mortgage because they have a place that is far too large for their needs. If they would reduce the size of their home and increase their land size, they would be better off for the purposes of self-reliance. Often it is a

"Keep Up With The Jones's" syndrome and it is a shame. A big house, fancy cars, and a need to impress others is not a formula for success, especially if you are trying to become less dependent on others.

It gives you a good feeling to have zero debt. It is not easy, but I proved it can be done. It takes time, effort, and many trade-offs. Only you can make it happen.

Investments

When most people think of investments, they think of stocks and bonds, IRAs, 401Ks, etc. I personally have a different view of investments. First, let me say right up front, I AM NOT an investment consultant, nor have I played one on television. I am not providing any recommendations in regard to the personal investment of your money, only presenting my perspective on the subject.

My father always told me to beware of the middleman. He who gets his share, no matter how you are affected, can't be good for you. As an example, a stockbroker gets a commission when you buy a stock, and gets another commission when you sell the stock. This commission has no relationship to how the stock does while you own it. Whether the stock goes up, or goes down, the stockbroker makes money, which comes out of your profits, or losses.

Our government works the same way with taxes. You do the work, then you pay a portion of what you earn, to them. If you invest it, and are lucky enough to make a profit, you then get to give more to the government in taxes. If you buy something, you get to pay additional sales tax to a government agency. At the same time, because of irresponsible spending of tax dollars, and the lack of a budget to control that spending, our money is being devalued more each day. Never forget Germany after WWI when they needed a wheelbarrow full of paper money to buy a loaf of bread.

Unfortunately, it is difficult to invest as a means to grow assets which in the end are worth less because of inflation. My idea of investing is to preserve what I already have, and avoid having that eroded by inflation.

One of those areas is precious metals. Gold and silver will always be worth something, and have never been worth nothing. But if you invest in precious metals, do so with the idea that it may have to be used as a means of trade or barter. I know people who buy one ounce gold pieces, but in reality, it will be difficult to trade or barter with a coin that is worth over twelve hundred dollars, unless there is something big you need. I have always found that one-tenth ounce gold pieces are more practical for that type of a situation. Silver can be considered in the same realm as gold. Many smaller denomination coins might be easier to use for buying goods if paper money doesn't work or exist.

Keep in mind that a time could come when the owning of gold or silver is regulated, or even prohibited by the government. I have had some younger people indicate that such a prohibition is very unlikely. Yet in 1933 the Emergency Banking Act made it illegal for American citizens to physically own gold. All gold was confiscated by the government. It was not until 1974 that the act was repealed, again allowing American citizens to own gold. Keep in mind that the reason for the act was a great depression, and I keep hearing that our current depression is the worst since the Great Depression. This has to make you think, and act with caution.

I have always found that certain investments never depreciate or go down in price. One of these is quality tools. I have tools that were owned by my grandfather and father and it is difficult to find tools to equal them today. My grandfather always told me as a child, buy the best tools you can afford, get the best quality, and buy them once. If you buy cheap junk, you will be buying those tools the rest of your life. I have never forgotten those words and even though the price of tools keeps going up, it seems the quality keeps going down.

Now, I certainly am NOT suggesting or recommending that you run out and take all your money out of the bank or cash in your IRA. But, as with all self-reliant strategies, be prudent and don't put all your eggs in one basket.

If you invest, do so wisely, with a thought to the future. If everything goes well, all investments will do fine. But, if the bottom falls out and our money is worthless, have some alternatives to help get you through.

Caching

The caching of valuables has occurred forever. Everybody has heard about buried treasures. This is still an effective means to protect valuables from theft, and fire. It basically entails you placing your valuables in some type of a waterproof container and burying it. It may sound archaic, but I find that it is a good way to hide things.

First of all, it is not fool proof, as someone could always accidentally find your cache. For that reason, again, I never recommend putting all your eggs in one basket. I prefer to place a small amount of valuables in many different caches. If one is found, you don't lose everything.

There are many types of devices you can use for caching, but I find small containers are best, unless you are caching some large items. I use caches mainly for cash, precious metals, and other small valuables, so they do not have to be secured in the home and be accessible to theft or fire.

Two preferred containers for smaller caches are metal ammo cans and PVC pipe. I prefer those made from PVC pipe as I can make them the size I need, which are usually small.

The author shows a good size cache tube made from PVC and ends. It can be used to hold cash, precious metals, or other small valuables

Whatever type of waterproof container you decide to use, prepare the contents of the cache container. I like to place my valuables in a heavy vacuum seal bag and vacuum seal it. Include a desiccant in the bag before sealing. After adding the bag to the container, add some more desiccants. Make sure the seal on the container is tight and waterproof.

Keep in mind that I do not cache stuff in hopes of leaving it there for a hundred years. Caching is used as a means to hide and protect the contents. When you need the contents, you need them. Don't bury them far from where you are if you might need the contents in an emergency.

Be careful that you don't place them in an area out of your control as things can change overnight. That new road starts going in through those beautiful woods down the road, and you only notice it as a piece of heavy equipment is observed digging in the area your cache was buried. Another reason to have many small caches, as opposed to one large one, is if you don't have a large piece of land, you might have to use someone else's. However, keep in mind that if you don't have control of the property, your cache is subject to loss.

If you are concerned that you might have to bug-out, or leave the area, in an emergency situation, you might want to have a cache or two buried in the area you intend going to, or one on the route taking you there. Again, all caches are subject to being found by those who do not own them. Cache with caution and be willing to lose what has been cached.

Bartering

Bartering has been a means of exchange long before we had currency. Basically, bartering is a system of exchange whereby goods or services are exchanged for other goods or

services without using a currency, e.g., money. Having a currency
has made it easier for people to trade goods, but if that means of
exchange disappeared, bartering would again be the way for people
to obtain what they need. However, keep in mind that bartering
can be a medium of exchange even if currency does exist.

We have already discussed both skills and extra supplies,
earlier in this book. and they will both be your bartering options.
Skills will go a long way. If someone needs something your skills
can provide, then you have something to barter with. If somebody
needs a sheath for a knife or a holster for a gun, I know I can
provide that. If they need a porch fixed or something built, I know
I can provide that as well. Now what does the other person have
that I need and is willing to trade for my skills. This is why skills
are so important, because many people don't have them.

On the other hand, if you have extra supplies, you can
barter for other supplies, or for skills that you don't have. There
are many lists out there that will tell you what will be the most
important items to have for barter if something catastrophic
happens, but nobody really knows what will be important to other
people if that did indeed happen.

I try to look at it as a "needs" thing and everybody's needs
are different. But there are certain things that everybody either
needs or wants. Although alcohol and tobacco both have high
health risks, they are also comfort items during stressful times.
They would both be good barter items.

Food will always be a need and therefore good for
bartering. If you have a garden, you have a renewable barter item.
Grow more than you need and barter the rest. The same can be
said for eggs, if you have chickens.

People always need shelter and warmth. Clothes and blankets will always be on a need list. This is also where the skill of sewing comes in. You can always produce, or repair, items that can be bartered. Firewood is another item that works well for barter.

I could go on listing things, but you get the idea. All the things that we need or have kept extra supplies of, are also needed by other people. Keep bartering in mind when you need something you don't have, and have things that other people don't.

PART 3
OTHER BASIC NEEDS

Chapter 10
<u>Water Is Essential</u>

As everyone knows, water is essential for life. Therefore, a self-reliant person will ensure that water is available, or attainable. Don't fool yourself into thinking that as long as you are on a public water system that water will always come out of the faucet. Also, if you have your own well, unless you have a means to pump the water out of the well, you won't have water.

Obtaining Water

In order to be self-reliant you will need a reliable supply of water. Water for drinking must be potable, but you will also need water for cleaning, gardening, etc., which does not. If you live in a city or an area where you must rely on a public water system, you are at the mercy of that system for a constant supply. However, if that supply fails, such as a water main break, contamination, or an emergency situation, you may have to rely on the water stored in your hot water heater, or water that you have stored in another manner, such as bottles, barrels, etc.. However, you can also collect rain water and that will be discussed shortly.

If you have access to streams, ponds, lakes, etc, you should always have a means to collect water. But you will need to purify that water before you drink it, and that will be addressed in this chapter as well. However, if the water will be used for a garden, then it can be collected and used right from the source. As a backup plan, I have a small portable 12 volt water pump that can be taken to a water source, and using two hoses and a 12 volt battery, I can fill water containers in the event that was necessary.

If you are not in an area where you must rely on a public water system, you will need your own well. Most wells run off electricity, and I have a back-up generator which also runs my well when the power goes out. But that generator relies on a non-renewable energy source, gas. For a long term situation without power, or for property that has a well but no electricity, a hand pump can be the way to go. There are various manufacturers who make hand pumps for shallow wells, but what if you have a deep well?

There is a company called Bison Pumps® and they specialize in manufacturing Deep Well Hand Pumps which can access depths of 300 feet. These pumps can also be used to pressurize a tank. They are made in the United States with all stainless construction and a lifetime warranty. I am seriously considering getting one of these as a back-up for our well.

This is a view of a Deep Well Hand Pump made by Bison Pumps.
They are made in the U.S. with all stainless steel construction.
Photo used with permission and provided by Bison Pumps.

Of course there are other ways to power your well such as wind and solar power. These will be discussed further in Chapter 12 - Alternate Power.

Collecting Rain Water

In a suburban or country area, if you own a home, you will normally have gutters that can be used to divert rain water to some type of collection container.

We use rain barrels that were designed for that purpose, as well as some 55 Gallon drums. We place them under the gutter downspouts on the house, garage, and potting shed. All together we have four seventy-five gallon and three fifty-five gallon barrels, which provide us with a total of Four Hundred and sixty-five gallons of water for our various gardens. In an emergency, of course this water could also be filter and purified for drinking.

These are two 75 gallon water barrels at the front corner of the garage and are connected together, whereby the barrel on the left overflows into the barrel on the right.

These two barrels are at the rear corner of the author's garage. Both are 55 gallons and a hose between the barrels allows both to stay relatively equal with water. As you dispense from the front barrel the second barrel refills the first through the siphon effect.

Sometimes you have to get creative in order to collect enough water. I have a 75 gallon water barrel at the rear of the potting shed, which is closest to the vegetable garden. At first I only had a gutter on the front side of the roof, but because of the small size of the roof, it didn't always fill the barrel when it rained. I added an additional gutter on the back side of the potting shed and directed both gutter downspouts to the same 75 gallon water barrel. Between the two downspouts, they now fill the barrel much faster.

The above photos show the dual gutter and downspout system
on the author's potting shed.

As indicated, we have various rain barrels around our residence as well. We typically collect rain water for our gardens. However, if you intend to collect water from your gutters for the purpose of drinking, you will need to get more creative. There are special devices such as Sloped screens that divert debris from the downspout, and "first-flush" diverters that divert the initial water through the system to reduce debris. They then allow the water to continue to your collection device. Because of various roofing materials, as well as other variables, I would recommend purifying the water to make it potable.

Many people in the country, like myself, use rain barrels, as described above, to collect water. However, there are other individuals who live in an apartment or condominium, and don't have the luxury of connecting into a gutter and down spout system, due to regulations or lease agreements. However, it would be handy to be able to collect some rain water.

Giving this some thought I was reminded how many times, while camping up in the Adirondack Park, I used a tarp to collect and channel rain water to bottles and pots. This got me to thinking, and I figured if someone had just a small piece of ground, they could setup some type of pole system that would allow them to quickly deploy a tarp to collect and channel water to a five gallon bucket. The poles could stay up, but the tarp could be deployed or removed in a moment.

The following is the result of an experiment I did to test this idea. I used four fence T-posts, one 8 foot x 10 foot tarp, one five gallon bucket, some small diameter cordage, and one rock. Once the posts were set, and loops were tied onto the tarp, I was able to deploy the system in less than a minute, and take it down just as fast. It should be noted that a similar configuration could be developed that would allow someone who had a balcony to do the same type of thing. You can also experiment with different sized tarps and different post heights.

I used T-posts for the four uprights because they have tabs that stick out and up, on all but the bottom section. On the bottom, there are a couple of tabs that stick out and down, and I used this as an advantage to keep the tarp taut. When placing the posts in the ground, make sure that the tabs are facing inward! The rear two T-posts are just slightly wider than the width of the 8 foot width of the tarp, whereby with the loops attached, the tarp could be attached taut at the upper tabs on each side.

The front two T-posts are placed 10 feet ahead of the rear posts (or whatever the length of your tarp is), and are inset on each side. The amount of inset is determined by how much dip you want in the front of the tarp. In my case the front T-posts ended up being 4-1/2 feet apart which allowed the center of the dipped tarp to still sit above a five gallon bucket. Loops on front corners are also placed on the top tabs of T-posts. It should be noted that the tarp has five grommets on the end, and the center one will sit over the five gallon bucket with a line attached to a rock to hold it in the bucket. A line with a loop at the end is measured and attached to the other two grommets which are the second one in on each side, so that one on each side can be pulled down to a tab that sticks out but faces down. This ensures that the tarp stays taut and keeps the wind from blowing it around.

Waiting for the rain to test it, it only took three days, but I finally saw it coming. At first it was only a medium rain and the bucket was filling slowly. However, I could hear thunder and knew a heavier rain was coming, and it did. The first five gallon bucket filled in a matter of minutes and I ran and got another bucket that filled in two minutes. The rain continued very heavy for another ten minutes or so and I could have filled many more buckets.

This illustrates that with a medium rain, you will still be able to collect some rain water. But with a heavy down pour, you can fill bucket after bucket. This definitely shows the advantage of a system like this for gardening, or emergency needs. If you can't utilize the down spouts from your gutters, this might be an option.

This is a view of the four T-posts placed in the ground to hold the tarp for the quick deploying rain catchment system.

This shows the 8' x 10' tarp added to the T-posts using just loops on the tarp and tabs on the posts.

This shows the quick deploying rain catchment system during a heavy rain pouring water into the bucket.

If you are further interested in this quick deployment rain catchment system, I have an article showing many more photos at http://www.survivalresources.com/Articles/Quick_Deploying_Rain_Catchment.html, as well as a video

If you want to get really creative, you can actually make your own gutters. While at Ballenberg, Switzerland, a living history museum, we saw how they make gutters out of long pine trees. They cut off the top one-third, and using the bottom two-thirds and a tool called a "Gutter-Adze," they chop out a gutter like trough. They even used branches from trees to hold the gutters up to the side of the roof. In a country environment, this would be a great self-reliance project, and as soon as I got back from Switzerland I ordered a gutter adze, just in case.

This photo shows a gutter in Switzerland that was homemade from a pine log.

This photo shows that even the gutter brackets to hold up the homemade gutters in Switzerland were made from branches.

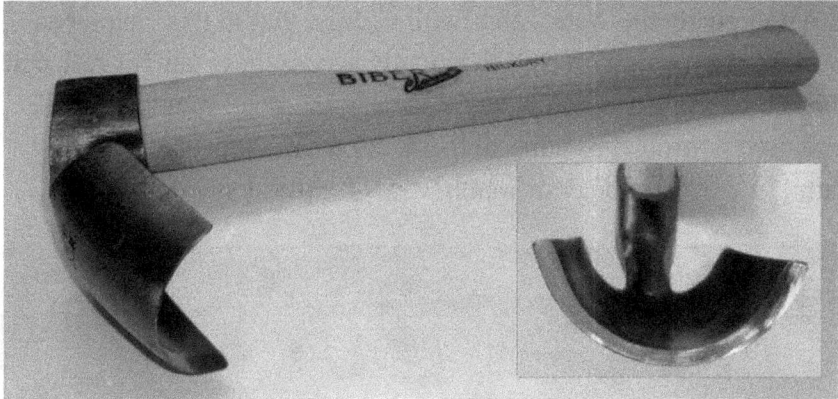

This is a view of the author's Gutter Adze, with an inset showing a close-up of the actual blade.

Before leaving the collection of rain water, I should mention snow. Snow can be collected and melted for both washing and drinking water. I have friends in Montana that use melted snow for all their water needs during those months they can't obtain water from any other source.

Obtaining Water In An Emergency

Keep in mind, in a city or urban area, in an emergency situation, water is often available on the outside of commercial buildings, but are protected by tamper resistant hose bibs. In order to access this supply, you will need a tool called a four way Sillcock Key. This will allow you to turn on the water, which is normally in a pressurized system. The water can be used to fill containers which can be taken to your home for use. Now I'm not suggesting that you just go and steal water from the outside of commercial buildings, but if you ask, you may be given permission.

If it is a real emergency, then you might have to do what is necessary to get water. If the local water supply is polluted, this will normally be announced on the radio. In that case, you will want to purify the water, and I will address that in this chapter as well. I did a video on how to actually access these tamper resistant hose bibs using a Sillcock key, as well as some of the doors that are used to protect or conceal them. You can view that video at http://www.youtube.com/watch?v=5N49iqRxnUo

This shows the size of a four-way Sillcock key, a tool used to access tamper-resistant hose bibs on the outside of commercial buildings.

Making Water Potable

If you are using water for your garden you don't need to be too concerned about it potability, but if you need it to drink, then this must be a consideration.

The water that comes into your home from a public water supply, or your own well, is normally potable water, meaning drinkable. Sometimes this water needs to be tested, but for the most part, it is potable.

However, water obtained from other sources may be contaminated with any of the four water-borne enteric pathogens; bacteria, viruses, protozoan cysts (such as Giardia or Cryptosporidium), and parasites. Contamination can also be caused by various other sources such as chemicals (chemical spills often contaminate water systems), radiation, etc.

For this reason, you should have various ways to filter and purify water. The first thing you should think about is pre-filtering. This does not purify the water, but it removes debris, bugs, and sediments that can clog a filter or purification device. You can use anything from a cotton bandana to a coffee filter. Basically, you want to get the water as clear as you can before attempting to filter or purify it.

The second thing you should understand is not all commercial devices are created equal. There are many Water Filters on the market that indicate they purify water but they don't. Most water filters only filter water, not purify it. And, although there are some units that both filter and purify water, most do not. Depending on the size of the filter (and you must check before buying), a filter will eliminate Protozoa (such as Giardia & Cryptosporidium), and most bacteria. They will not eliminate viruses or bacteria smaller than the size listed on the filter (normally 0.2 – 0.3 microns). Most Filters eliminate Protozoans (such as Giardi lamblia and Cryptosporidium), and most bacteria, but will not filter out viruses, such a Hepatitis A.

There are various portable devices that are used for camping and outdoor adventures and can be used for filtering and purifying water. They can be easily stored until needed. Although they are handy for an occasional emergency, they are not meant to be used as a full-time means to filter or purify water. They also are not useful against heavy metals, chemicals, or radiation.

This photo shows various water filters made by Katadyn which are good quality devices and are appropriate for a temporary situation.

This shows the author using a Katadyn pump filter to obtain water from a stream. Although a good way to obtain water during a short term emergency situation, it is not meant to be an everyday, permanent use, device.

Another way to purify water is by boiling it. Although this method does eliminate water-borne enteric pathogens, it does not eliminate heavy metals, chemicals, or radiation. It also requires a source of fuel to keep the water boiling.

For a more permanent situation you will need something that will process a higher quantity of water. At my home I have a UV system that purifies the water as it comes from the well. However, it relies on electrical power to operate. Without electricity, or a means of backup power (which we have) an alternative is necessary.

There are various gravity type water filters available commercially by companies such a Katadyn and Berkey. These are basically a container that has ceramic filters in it. This container sits on the top of another container. You pour water into the top container and as the water is drawn through the ceramic filters by gravity, the filtered water drips into the container below it. These type of filters can filter a lot of water with no effort on your part, other than filling the top container. They are slow, but again, you can be doing something else, while gravity does your work. Unfortunately, these systems cost $200 - $300.00.

I looked at several different models and then checked the internet and learned that I could make my own gravity filter using two five gallon buckets, a spigot, and three ceramic filters. I had to give it a try.

At first I looked at five gallon buckets at Home Depot made by Leaktite Corp. in Leominster, MA. The buckets had the HDPE-2 as a recycle symbol on the bottom, but they didn't say food grade. Most people don't worry about this in food buckets as they use Mylar bag liners. But this bucket was going to hold water, so I checked further.

Upon contacting Leaktite Corp., I was told unequivocally that their buckets were not "food grade" and were meant for paint and chemicals. I was told they did not recommend them for food, unless a Mylar bag was used inside. I asked about storing water in them and they said definitely not. I did some further research and apparently non food grade buckets can be made from recycled HDPE material and they use a mold release agent that can leach from the bucket into its contents. Food grade buckets use air pressure to release the bucket from the mold.

I was able to get some food grade five gallon buckets free from Dunkin Donuts. Next I needed filters and I found the replacement ceramic filters for the Berkey system at Amazon.com for $98.00 for four filters, which was perfect, as I needed three filters for this project, and one more filter for another project which I will discuss next. I also found the spigot at Amazon.com. Once everything arrived, I was ready to begin the project.

The first thing I did was mount the spigot at the bottom of one of the five gallon buckets, using a 3/4 inch hole. I mounted it so that the bucket could sit on a counter without the spigot hanging lower than the bucket.

I was using three ceramic filters in this system, so I made measurements on the bottom of the second bucket, and made three marks from the center to the outside rim 120 degrees from each other, providing me with three evenly spaced marks. I then drilled three 1/2 inch mounting holes for the ceramic filters.

I would also need three holes in the lid of the lower bucket, for the filters to stick through, so before mounting the filters in the top bucket, I placed the bottom of the filter bucket on the lid of the bottom bucket and used the holes I just drilled to mark the lid. I then used those marks to drill 1-3/8 inch holes in the bottom lid.

This shows the spigot mounted to the bottom of one of the five gallon buckets, and the bucket can sit without hitting the spigot.

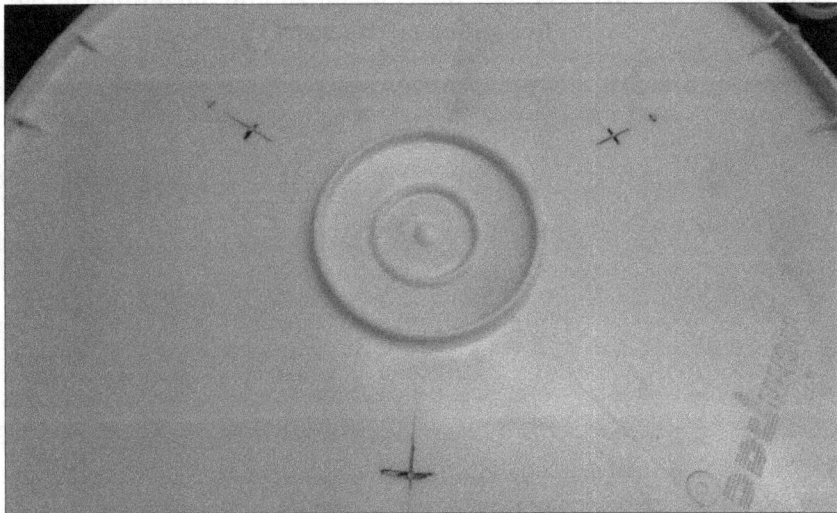

This shows the marks 120 degrees from each other on the bottom of the filter bucket for the ceramic filter mounting holes.

The filters were placed through the mounting holes from the inside of the top bucket, with the rubber gasket on the inside. The mounting nut was then tightened onto the portion of the filter that protruded through the bottom of the bucket, to hold the filters securely in place.

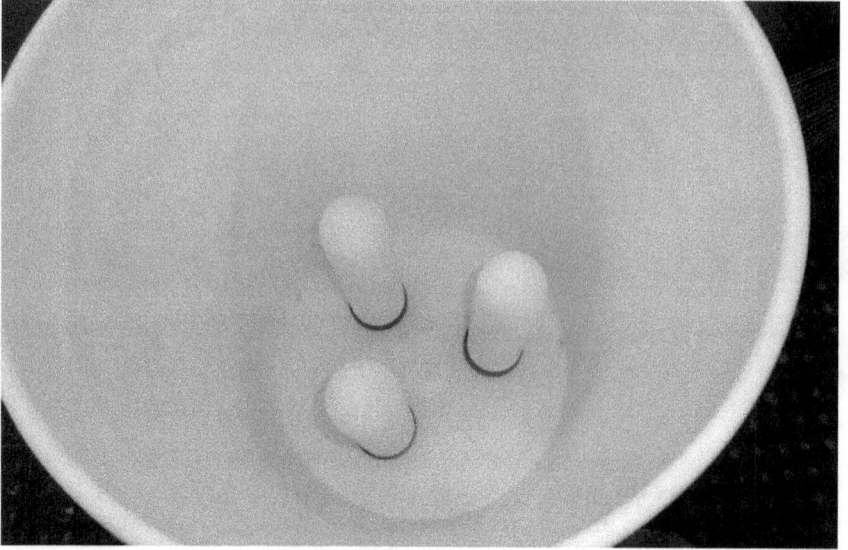

This shows the three ceramic filters mounted into the bottom of the five gallon top bucket.

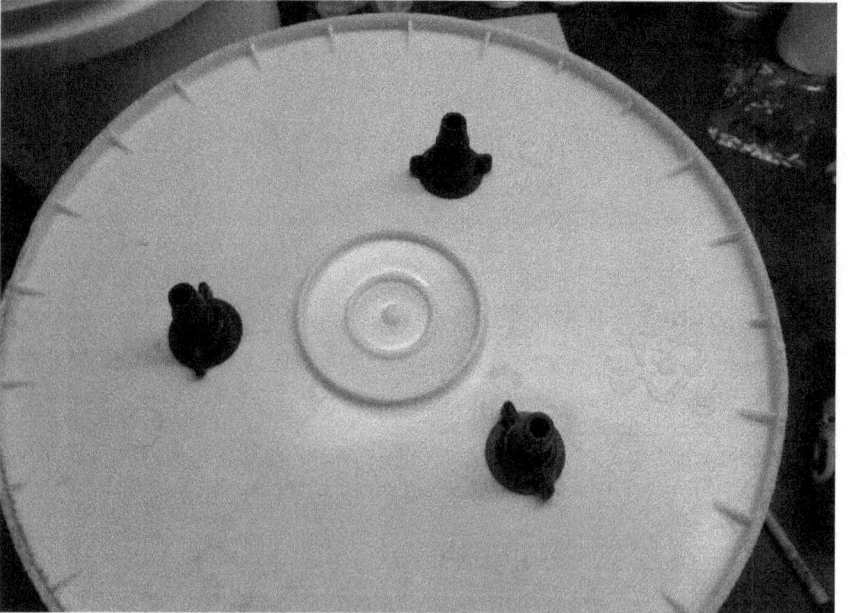

This is a view of the nuts on the bottom of the filter bucket that secured the ceramic filters to the inside of the bucket.

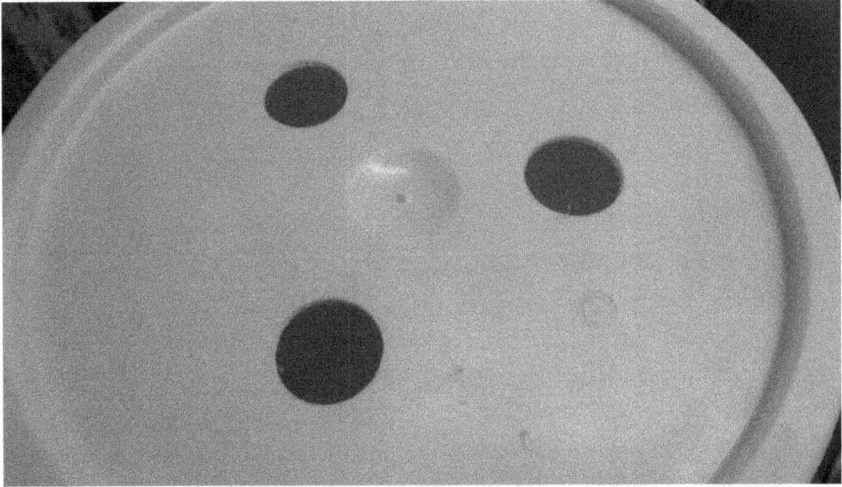

This shows the 1-3/8 inch holes in the lid of the lower bucket.

This shows the bottom catch bucket with lid in place.

The top bucket is now set on top of the lower bucket so that the ends of the ceramic filters protrude through the holes in the lid of the bottom bucket. You fill the top bucket with water, and slowly, it will filter into the bottom bucket. You can access the filtered water from the bottom bucket via the spigot at the bottom.

This is a view of the completed 5 Gallon Gravity Filter System.

The total cost for the five gallon gravity filter system was $77.95 (filters - $75.00, buckets - free, spigot - $2.95).

Although the above system has worked well, I wanted something smaller that I could set on the kitchen counter. I thought I would build the same type of system in a smaller, two gallon bucket, and use only one filter in the center. I knew this system would drip even slower than the five gallon system, but it could stay in the kitchen where it would be handy to use.

As you will recall, I had purchased a set of four ceramic filters for the five gallon project above, so I already had a ceramic filter for this project. I also had a spigot, as I had ordered two when ordering for the above system. Now all I needed were the buckets.

I couldn't find any food grade, two gallon, buckets locally, I was able to find some made by Plastican Inc. and they come with a certificate certifying them as being "Food Grade" and are approved under the Federal Food, Drug and Cosmetics Act, Title 21 CFR Section 177.1520, as free of animal based ingredients, as well as being free of Bisphenol A. I ordered them from Amazon.com.

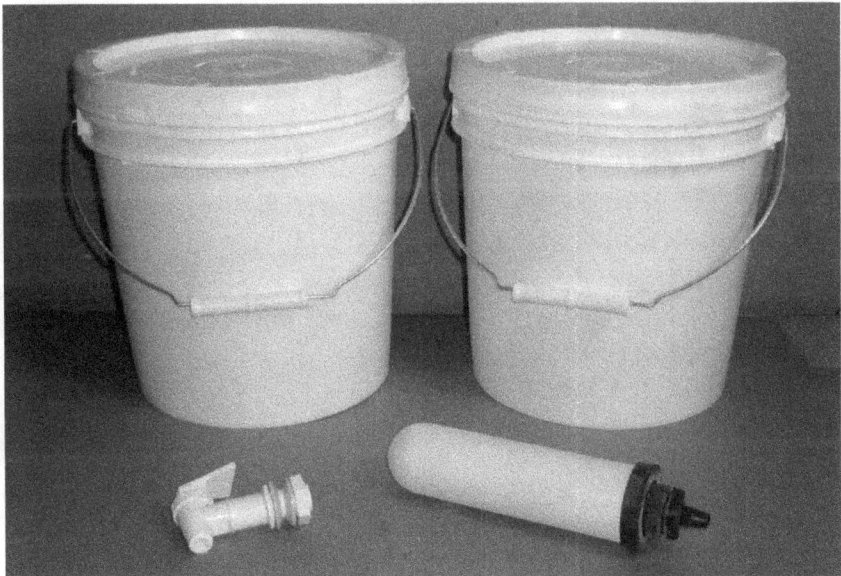

These are parts needed for the two gallon Gravity Filter system.

I started this project attaching the spigot to the bottom of one the two gallon buckets in the same manner as I had for the five gallon bucket. Again, I mounted it so that the bucket could sit flat on a surface, without hitting the spigot.

Because I was only using one filter, I would mount that in the center of the top bucket. I drilled the required 1/2 inch hole and mounted the ceramic filter in the bucket.

I also needed a 1-3/8 inch hole in the lid of the bottom bucket so the filter from the top bucket could protrude into the bottom bucket. This was accomplished and the system was ready to go.

The system indeed was much smaller, taking up a lot less room on a kitchen counter. This is now our primary use filter.

This shows the two gallon bucket with the single filter mounted in the center of the bottom.

This shows the size comparison between the two gallon and five gallon Gravity Filter systems on the kitchen counter.

Always wanting to be self-reliant, my wife and I discussed having a system that would handle more contaminants, such as heavy metals and chemicals. Even though we don't live near the ocean, we do live near a large river that is tidal, and a water distiller will also desalinate water. Distilled water can also be used in soap making, which my wife does, and for use in steam irons, and to refill lead-acid batteries (which could be part of a solar panel, wind turbine, or hydro power system).

The process of distilling water is called Thermo-Distillation, which means by heat. It removes the broadest range of contaminates of any water purifier, to include viruses, bacteria, cysts, and heavy metals. Real handy in an area like New Orleans, Louisiana, when they had their water badly contaminated. It is also my understanding that distillation can remove some radioactive materials (radionuclides), but not all. However, my thought is that even though you have removed some from the water, they do not disappear. Instead, they accumulate in the distiller and you will have to deal with them, and they are now in a concentrated form. How do you handle what is basically radioactive waste? I'm not sure, but this was not my reason for building a water distiller.

The concept of the Themo-Distillation is pretty simple. You place contaminated or salt water in a pressure cooking device. As the water boils, it creates steam. The steam travels through a tube to a coil that is placed in cold water. As the steam enters the coils, it condenses back to water that is now pure distilled water. Maybe an over simplification, but that's how it works.

I have seen various types of home-brew distillers in various articles and videos, but I had a few prerequisites for the distiller I wanted to build. I wanted it to be built as cheaply as possible using available materials and a little shop skill. I wanted it to be sturdy so it could be moved around and stored and not have it break apart. I wanted to be able to set it up easily for use, and then take it down easily for storage. Lastly, I wanted the pieces stackable so it could be easily stored.

After some planning, it was determined that we would need a pressure cooker, copper tubing, some brass fittings, silicone high temperature tubing, and a two gallon bucket with lid. My wife, Denise, and I started ordering parts. Although we have a couple of pressure cookers, we didn't want to use one of our good Swiss ones, and wanted one that we could dedicate to the project. Denise was able to find a Presto 6-Quart Stainless Steel pressure cooker on eBay for $28.00; a real good find. I was able to find the Copper Tubing, fittings, and 2 Gallon Bucket with Lid at Home Depot. The only thing left was the Silicone High Temperature Tubing, which I was able to find at a Home Brewing Store.

When we finally had all the parts in hand, I headed for the shop to start making the Condenser Coil for the Cooler Tank. I had a two gallon bucket that had an inside diameter of 8" at the bottom and 9" at the top, and the height was 9-1/2". I wanted the condenser coil to be smaller than the 8" bottom diameter, and the coil that came out of the box started at 11". I began carefully reworking the coil so that they would have an outside diameter of approximately 7". My plan was to use two quart frozen juice bottles in the center to assist in cooling, and this size coil would allow for that, and still be an inch or so away from the walls of the bucket.

When I completed the coil, I wasn't happy. When you set the coil up on end on the bench, gravity came into play and the coils would slowly start collapsing down on themselves. I wanted the coils to stay a predetermined space from each other and do so in a permanent manner. I also didn't want to suspend the coil from the top of the bucket, as it was my feeling that they would still wiggle around, and I wanted this thing rock solid.

I determined that if I made some type of frame where each coil could be attached at a specified distance, and somehow attach this frame to the bottom center of the bucket, it would be permanent and solid. Looking around I found some Punched Flat Bar made from zinc coated steel (available at Home Depot) and I thought this might just be what I was looking for. I was able to bend the flat bar into a "U" shape that would fit around the outside of the coils. I made sure that when I bent it, the holes on one side were slightly higher that the holes on the other. My idea was to use strong zip-ties to secure the coils to this "U" shaped frame. With the holes offset, this would ensure the coils continued in an upward spiral, which is necessary when the steam is condensed back to water and needs to flow down the coils. If one coil faces in an upward angle, or is higher than the one across from it, the water will not flow down, and this could also cause pressure to build up back to the pressure cooker.

The idea worked as planned, but it would not sit upright in the bucket. So I riveted a cross bar, made from the leftover Punched Flat Bar, on the bottom of the "U" shaped frame and this solved the problem. The Condenser coil was now ready to mount permanently into the cooler bucket.

I needed to mount the condenser coil in the two gallon bucket in a manner where the outlet tube at the bottom would protrude from the side of the bottom of the bucket, and the inlet tube at the top protruded from the top side of the bucket. I didn't want the inlet tube to stick up above the top of the bucket, because for storage, I wanted to be able to put the lid on the bucket and store the pressure cooker on top.

It was a little work, with some twisting and spinning, but I was able to get the outlet tube through an angled hole I made in the bottom side of the bucket. I then made a slot in the top side of the bucket so the inlet pipe could slide down into it. This required that

I use a piece of Kydex to hold the inlet tube in place. This I simply riveted to the upper side of the bucket. Once everything was in place, I used a quick-set two-part Epoxy to both secure, and waterproof, the inlet and outlet pipe to the bucket. I still had a little wiggle, so I mixed up some more Epoxy and secured the "X" shaped frame to the inside bottom of the bucket. When it dried, nothing moved and I finally had what I wanted. Once the epoxy dried, I tested the Cooler Tank to ensure that it was watertight and it did not leak around the inlet or outlet tubing. It was watertight and ready to go.

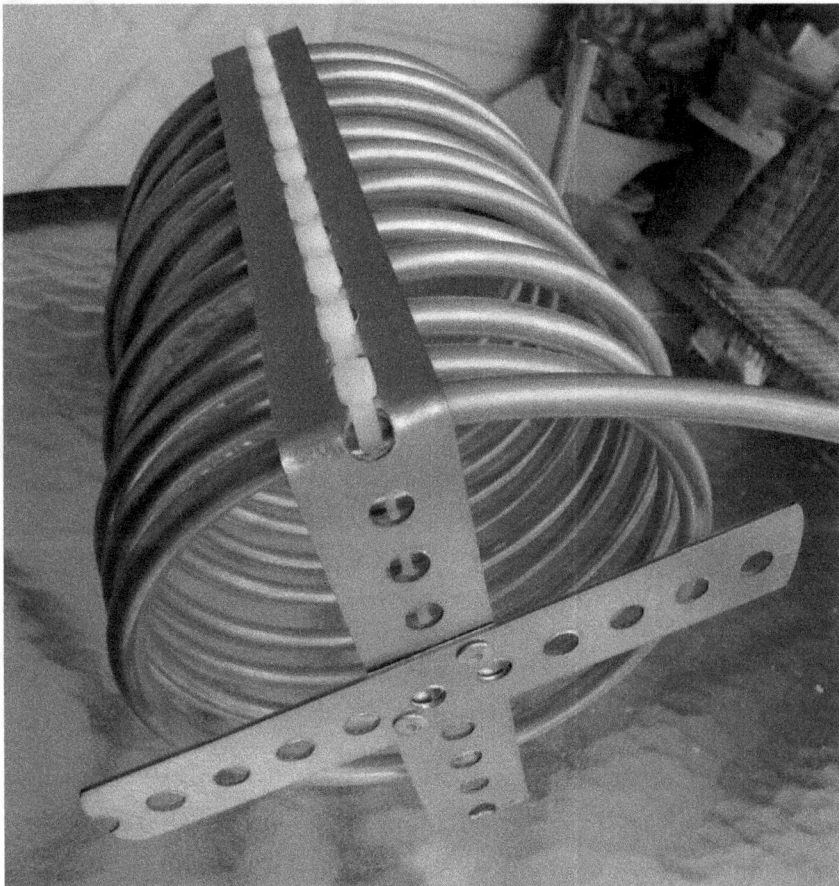

This is a view of the bottom of the completed condenser coil with the cross piece in place for stability.

**A view of the completed cooler tank with the condenser coil
mounted in the two gallon bucket.**

Once the Cooling Tank was complete, we ran a solution of
warm water and vinegar through it just to make sure the inside of
the copper tubing was clean. It was then rinsed with more warm
water.

Next, I had to remove the original pressure valve from the
top center of the pressure cooker lid, as it was too small. I replaced
it with a brass fitting that provided me with a 3/8" O.D. outlet to
accommodate the Silicone High Temperature Tubing.

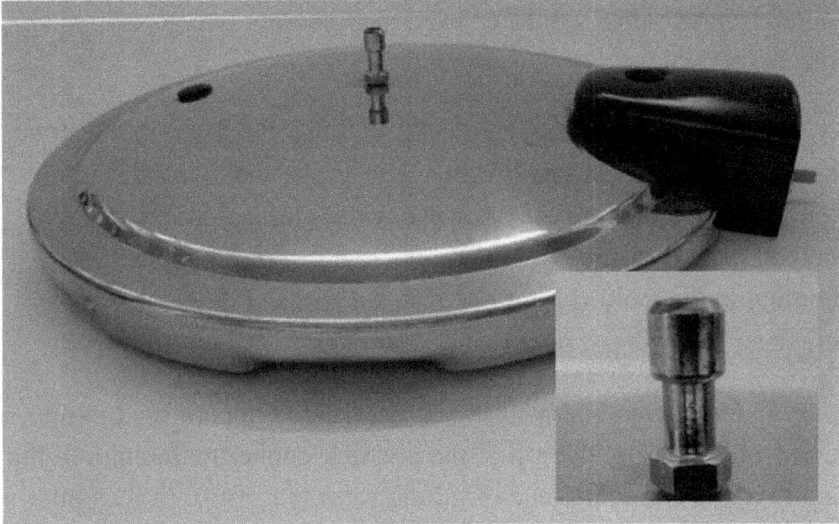

This is the pressure cooker lid with the original pressure valve.

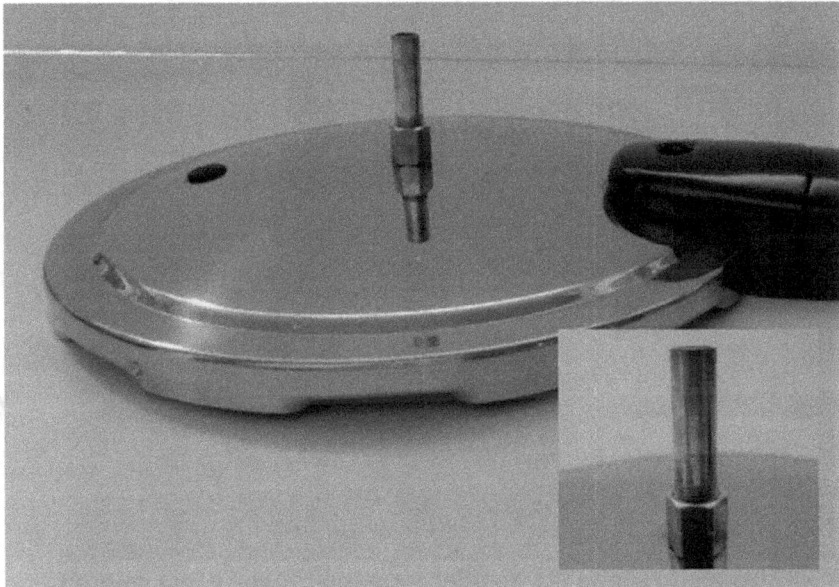

This shows the modified Pressure Cooker lid with the new, larger fitting for the 3/8" tubing.

Once all the parts were completed, it was time to test the system. It should be noted, that prior to completing the project, we had filled two, two quart juice bottles, with water and placed them in the freezer. They would be used in the cooler tank to help keep the water cool.

The pressure cooker was set on the left burner on the stove and filled, two-thirds, with water. The cooler tank was placed on the counter to the right of the stove, which left an unused burner between the pressure cooker and the cooling tank. I knew the cooling tank would get hot once we started, so I didn't want to add any heat by setting it next to a hot burner.

I now cut a piece of the silicone high temperature tubing that would fit from the top of the pressure cooker to the inlet of the cooler tank. Another piece of tubing was cut to fit from the outlet of the cooler tank to a two quart bottle we placed on the floor below the cooler tank.

This photo shows the distiller setup on the stove and counter.

The pressure cooker was heated and as the water began to boil you could see steam starting to enter the tubing above the lid. At this point we placed one of the frozen bottles in the cooling tank and filled it with cold water. We watched the process and it continued with steam being sent to the cooler tank inlet, the steam was then condensed back to water which exited the outlet pipe, and ran down the tubing to the bottle on the floor.

Now I must warn you that watching this process is like watching grass grow. The water in the cooler tank started to heat up and we had to replace the frozen bottle with another one. After the second one melted, we just used cold water in the bottles. Keep in mind that the cooler tank does get hot as well as the inlet and outlet pipes, so be careful that you don't touch them.

It took two and one half hours to almost fill the two quart bottle on the floor. So as you can see the process is slow, it takes a lot of fuel, and you need a continual source of cold water to keep the cooling tank cool. But you have distilled water.

To store the system, we simply place the inlet and outlet hose in zip-closure freezer bags and store them inside the pressure cooker. We have rubber caps to place over the inlet and outlet of the cooler tank, as well as the outlet on the lid of the pressure cooker. We place the lid on the cooler tank and then place the pressure cooker on top. It can now be stored on a shelf until it is needed.

I have an article at SurvivalResources.com under DIY articles which shows many more photos of the construction of the distiller. If you are interested, you can check it out further there.

Because of the need for fuel and cooling water, I am now looking into building a Solar Distiller, which will utilize the sun for the heat, instead of fuel. It looks something like a solar oven, but it collects water that evaporates on the inside of a glass lid, that is at an angle. The water then runs down the glass by gravity and collects in a small trough that directs it outside of the box into a container. This is a very interesting concept and I will be constructing one in the near future.

Desalination

Although we discussed the distiller in the above section, which can be used to desalinate salt water, I wanted to note that there are devices made for the sole purpose of desalinization.

There are various companies that make industrial sized desalinators, but for portable use, the best I have found are made by Katadyn in Switzerland. They have a small portable unit called the Katadyn Survivor 06, which is hand operated and is the smallest in the world. It is compact and lightweight and is trusted by militaries and individuals around the globe. While my wife and I were taking a tour of the Katadyn Factory in Switzerland, we actually got to watch them assembling this desalinator, which is done by hand, and it is really a robust unit.

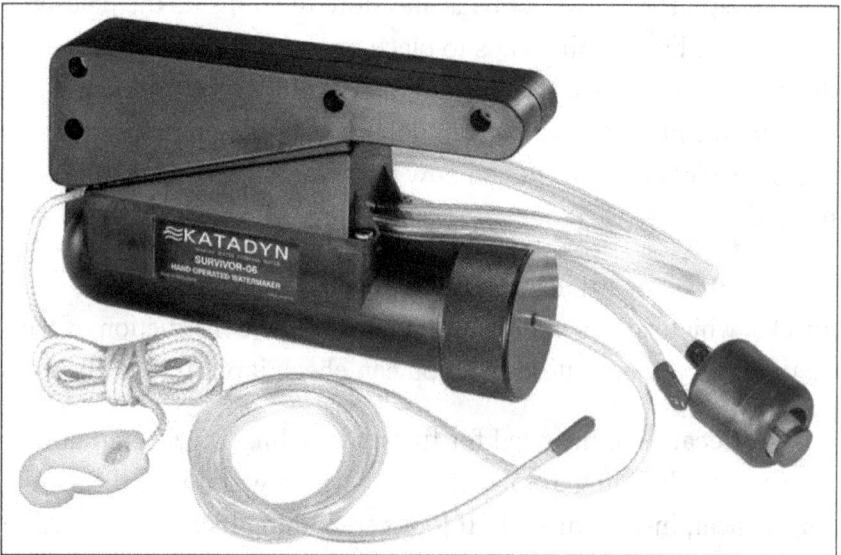

This is a view of the Katadyn Survivor-06 hand-held desalinator.
Photo courtesy of Katadyn North America

Katadyn also produces some desalinators that can be powered by both 12 and 24 volts, which make them idea for being powered off a solar powered system. These type units would come in handy if your lived near salt water, especially in an emergency.

Water Storage

There are various ways to store water for your needs. However, even though you can never have too much water, storing water is limited by the amount of room you have to store it. If you have a small place, such as an apartment, the amount of water you store will be much less than if you had abundant space.

With that being said, there are various ways to store water, and this will be divided into Drinking water, and water used for cleaning, gardening, etc. Even if you have public water, it could stop running. Therefore, you should, at least, have some drinking water stored for those times.

Drinking water can be as simple as having a case or two of bottled water in a closet, under a bed, etc. Bottled water can be kept up to five years. You should then use it and replace with a fresh supply.

There are a whole selection of water containers that are designed specifically for storing water. They range in size and can be purchased at various camping or preparedness stores. Reliance Products makes various sized containers for storing water and are available even at Wal-Mart.

I have found that the 2.5 Gallon size made by Scepter in Canada are the handiest for our needs. Although they make a 5 Gallon size, as you get older it is much easier to carry a 2.5 gallon in each hand as opposed to trying to lug the five gallon size. We find you can easily store a couple in the back of a closet with little problem.

These are two, 2.5 Gallon (10-L), water containers by Scepter in Canada which the author uses to store water.

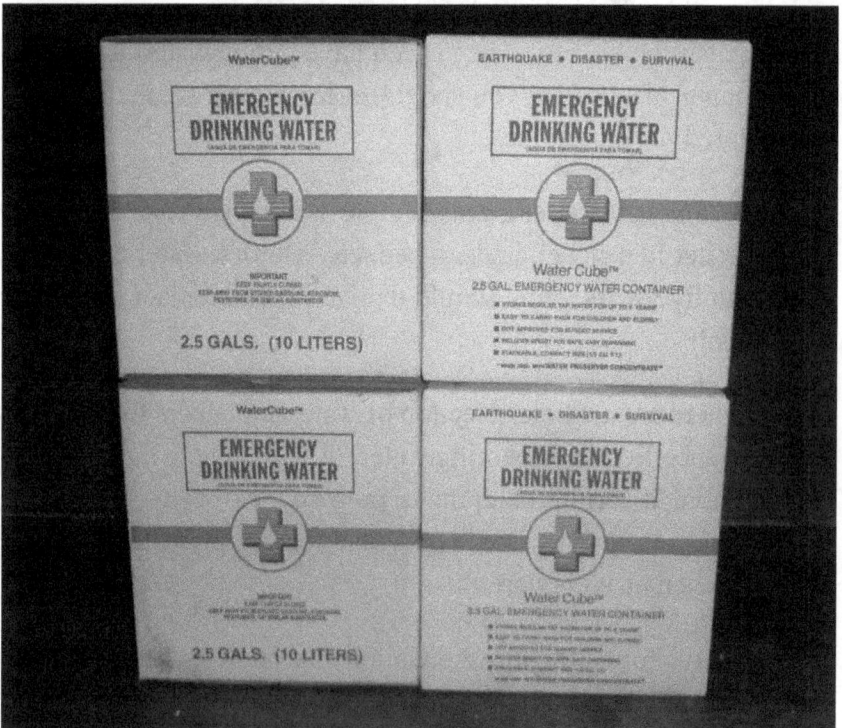

This shows a stack of four Water Cubes, which hold 2.5 Gallons of water each. They can be used to store water in a closet, etc.

Another product that is available, which is really handy for storing extra water is called the Water Cube™. Basically they are cardboard boxes with a food grade bladder (like that in a box of wine) that holds water. They have a spigot inside the box that can be screwed onto the neck of the bladder, and it can be set on its side for dispensing. There is an area on the box to record up to six dates when they were filled.

I like the Water Cube™ because they are stackable and can be easily stored in a closet or corner. If you have room like me, you can fill a whole shelf with them and this will provide you with potable water for a while. They are available from 7C's Safety & Environmental, Inc.

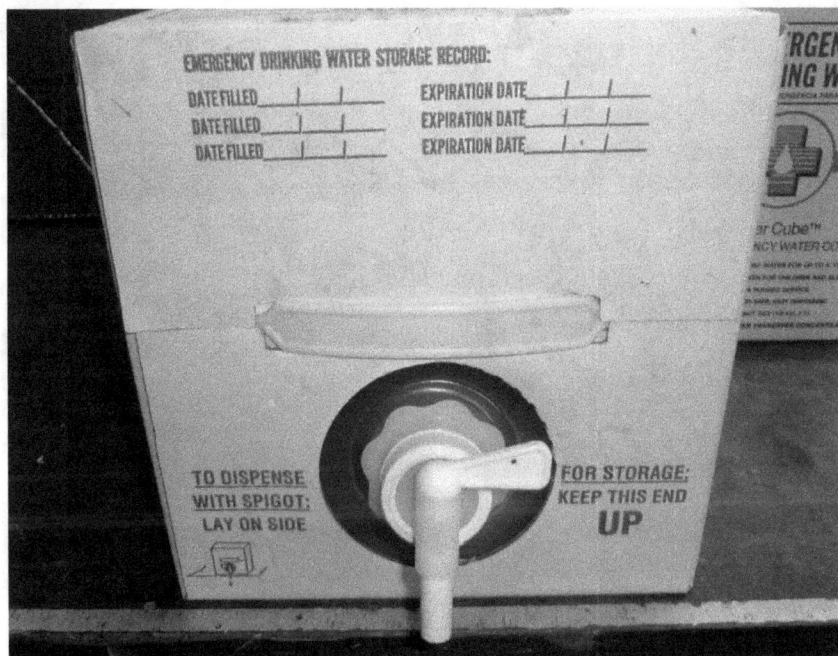

This shows the spigot that is stored inside the Water Cube, and can be attached when needed. Also note the area to record the various storage dates.

Another option is five-five gallon Food Grade barrels, which are also available at many emergency supply stores. They are handy for storing a lot of water, but keep in mind that they are very difficult to move when full. Put them where you want them before filling.

If you have a large area to store water, or you need to store all of your potable water, then a larger container will be required. I have seen various types and shapes, but I like the food grade containers that have a metal cage-type frame around them.

This is a 275 Gallon Food Grade Storage Tank that can be used to store water. Photo courtesy of Alvin Davis

This helps protect the container, and allows you to stack them (you will need some heavy equipment to lift them if they are full of water). They come in various sizes and you are only limited by space. I show a photo of a 275 Gallon Food Grade Storage Tank on the previous page.

If you are going to store water for any length of time in containers, and it is not chlorinated public water, you should add some chlorine to it to ensure it does not get contaminated. You can use any non-scented household chlorine bleach (5% sodium hypochlorite).

If the water is clear, add one-eighth teaspoon (8 drops) per gallon of water. If the water is cloudy, add one-quarter (16 drops). Make sure you slosh the water around and get some on the threads of the cap to ensure nothing grows there.

As you can see, there are a lot of options for storing Potable water. But if you only need to have water for gardening, cleaning, etc, you have many more options, as the containers do not have to be Food Grade. You are only limited by your imagination for watertight containers that can hold water for you non-potable needs. Earlier we discussed rain catchment barrels and these are a good start.

Cisterns

Cisterns are basically large waterproof containers used to hold and store water. Often, these cisterns were built into the ground, using stone or bricks, and were built more like a well. However, you had to fill them.

There are large cisterns available commercially for various rain catchment systems. They are beyond the scope of this book, but are worth some research.

There was an excellent article in "Home Power" magazine showing how a "Whole-House Water System can be designed and implemented in various configurations.

Earlier in this chapter I showed some gutters that were made in Switzerland. While exploring those, I saw one system where the gutters were directed to an underground cistern.

This photo shows a gutter system in Switzerland that directs all water from the roof to a covered cistern for storage.

The cistern held a large amount of water and there was an access door on one side. The water was obtained using buckets.

A system like this could be built today using solar, or other alternate power to pump the water to where it was needed. Even an irrigation system could be devised utilizing the water from the cistern.

As this chapter has illustrated, water is essential, and being able to obtain, purify, and store it is an important aspect of self-reliance.

Chapter 11
<u>Let There Be Light</u>

In this chapter, I will discuss various non-electrical lighting options for self-reliance. I will discuss electrical lighting methods, to include solar, in Chapter 12 - Alternate Power.

Candles

I have found that most people keep candles around in the event of a power failure. They are handy, and easy to use, as long as you have a way to light them. This gives you good reason to always keep a supply of matches or lighters around, as we discussed in Chapter 8 - Just In Case Supplies.

This shows various types of candle holders for both stick and votive candles, which make candles much safer to use.

Many people have "Stick" candles, as they are the type most used for a dinner table, etc. Another type of candle that is often kept around the house is "Votive" candles. These are small round candles, usually for ambiance. If you are going to use these types of candle, make sure you also have some candle holders for them. Holders make them much safer to use in the home.

Another type of candle that is very useful for lighting is a "Jar Candle." They come in many shapes and sizes and I find them handy because they are safer than an open flame candle. Another advantage of a jar candle is when you want to put it out, you simply place the lid on the jar and it extinguishes the candle.

This is a view of various sizes of Jar Candles that the author uses.

Candle Lanterns

Another handy way to use candles in the home is to use a candle lantern. The best I have found are made by Industrial Revolutions, and are called the UCO. They have a large lantern that uses three UCO candles. It has a spring mechanism in each candle tube that keeps pushing the candle up as it is used. I like this lantern because it gives off plenty of light, yet if you want less, you don't have to light all three candles, only as many as you need.

There is also the "Original" UCO candle lantern that collapses down when not in use. To use, just pull the top up, which reveals the glass globe. It uses one UCO candle and has the same spring mechanism as the Candlelier lantern. It also has an optional oil insert, whereby you can use lamp oil instead of the candle. Both of the UCO lanterns have a bail and a chain so they can be hung for use, or they can sit directly on a table.

I collect various old type lanterns, and one that I have is called the "Stonebridge" Automatic Folding Lantern, and it uses one large candle. It folds flat when not in use and has mica windows instead of glass. It was patented in 1903, and although rare, they are still useful for providing light. The company has been out of business for a long time, but a replica is currently being made and this is the one I have. It is offered by Garrett Wade.

This shows the author's UCO Candlelier and Original Lanterns, the oil insert for the Original, and the old "Stonebridge" lantern.

Making Candles

Making your own candles can be an easy and simple task, and for the purpose of self-reliance, they will be much cheaper than store bought candles.

I make both paraffin and beeswax candles and try to keep it simple. Paraffin can be purchased at craft stores, or stores that sell canning supplies (paraffin is often use to seal jams and jellies when canning). It normally comes in a one pound box and has four bars inside. Beeswax, I normally have to get from a candle making supply store. I like beeswax candles as they as they release negative ions which reduce the positive charged pollutants in the air to include pollen, dust, etc. We also recycle all our old used candles and place them in a bag. We re-melt them for making new candles, so the color is always a surprise.

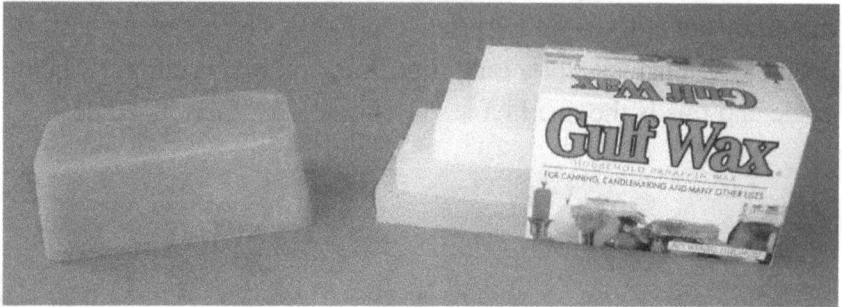

The left side of the photo shows a one pound block of beeswax and the right a one pound box of paraffin.

Although you can certainly make your own wicks by soaking plain cotton string in paraffin, I usually purchase the free standing type at craft stores. I like these as they have a small round metal base which keeps them standing upright when making your candles. They come in various lengths and package sizes.

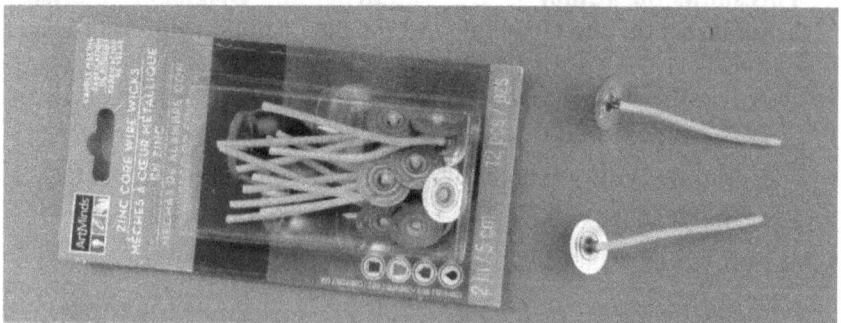

This shows a package of free standing wicks on the left and a view of two individual wicks at the right.

One of the types of candles I make, utilizes a small waxed milk carton, for the mold. I made this type of candle when I was a very young boy in the Cub Scouts. The only down side is that you normally have to tear the carton off the finished candle, so you need a supply of cartons. If you buy milk in the carton anyway, just save them and recycle them into candles.

I often use the smaller cartons, and cut off the folding top part, But you can use any size you want. To ensure that the wick stays in the middle, when pouring the paraffin or beeswax into the carton, I use a small piece of wood. This piece of wood has a slot on each end which sits over the carton keeping it square. There is a small hole in the center that allows the free standing wick to stick up and through the hole. These are very easy to make using a scrap piece of wood, or even a stick.

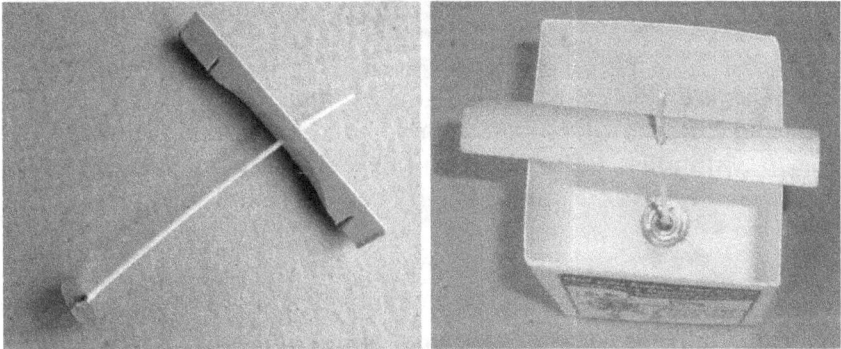

The left photo shows the small piece of wood the author made to keep the wick in the center of the carton mold. The slots fit over the edges of the carton. The right photo shows the holder in place.

Once you get your mold complete, It is time to melt some paraffin or beeswax. I do this with a simple double boiler, using an old small pot on the stove with a inch or two of water in it. I then turn the stove on to start heating the water.

I then use a coffee can sitting in the larger pot. Before I place the coffee can in the pot, I use pliers to bend a small pour spout on the edge, making it easier to pour from, once the paraffin or beeswax is melted.

This is a view of the author's double boiler using a small pot and coffee can. Note the pour spout on the coffee can made with pliers. The paraffin in the coffee can has a color because the author is recycling old candle pieces.

It should be noted that you must use Caution when melting the paraffin or beeswax. It does not boil, it will just keep getting hotter, and can actually combust. Once it is liquid it is ready and should be used. Turn the flame on the stove off. Also, don't drip it on you as it can cause a serious burn.

When it is ready to pour into the mold, carefully do so. I also suggest you lay down some newspaper, or cardboard, under the molds, in the event you drip some. Pour carefully, and slowly, so you do not move the wick around. You can fill the carton almost to the top, or, as I often do with the leftover melted paraffin or beeswax, I fill one with what is left and just have a shorter candle.

The above photo, from left to right, shows an empty milk carton, the carton with the folded top cut off, and the carton filled with paraffin. When the paraffin is cooled, the carton is simply torn off.

This shows a finished small milk carton candle on the left, and a shorter one on the right made from the leftover melted paraffin.

You will note in the photo above that there is an indentation in the carton candles. This often happens, because as the paraffin or beeswax dries, it shrinks in the center, which is the last to cool. You can melt some more paraffin or beeswax and add it into the indentation, just before it cools completely. Myself, I don't bother as I actually like the indentation. When I use the candle, the indentation makes sure that melted wax does not run over the side.

Next, I will show you how I make round candles. Again, there are molds available, but I make my own using PVC pipe and end caps. You can make them any diameter that PVC pipe is available. For the purpose of this tutorial, I am using a small, 5/8 inch O.D. diameter, which will make a small round candle. You will also need two end caps, a wick slightly longer than the candle length, and some duct tape.

The first thing is to cut the PVC pipe to the length you want the candle, and then cut the pipe in half, lengthwise. One of the end caps will be used for the bottom, and the second you will cut off the actual cap so that you have just a ring left.

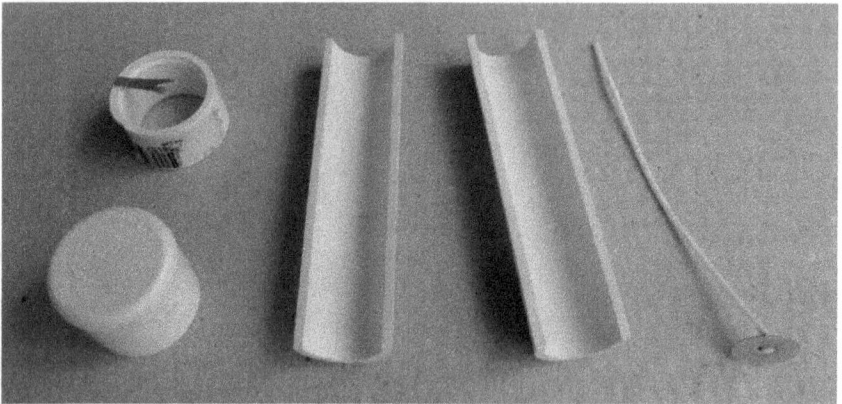

This shows the parts for the mold for a round candle made with PVC pipe and a free standing wick.

On the ring that you make from the second end cap, you can use a piece of old soda or beer and can cut a small strip. You then cut a small "V" in the strip, bend it ninety degrees and, using a small piece of duct tape, tape it to the side of the ring. Make sure that the center of the "V" is in the center of the tube. This will hold the wick at the center when pouring in the paraffin or beeswax.

Next you tape the PVC pipe back together using just enough duct tape to go around once. You then twist the bottom end cap in place. The ring you made is then place over the top. You are now ready to fill the pipe with melted paraffin or beeswax. As it starts to cool, you will probably need to add more melted paraffin or beeswax, as the center top tends to retract and you will have a hollow center.

The top left photo shows the PVC pipe duct taped together. The bottom left shows the end cap on the bottom and the top ring, with the wick holder, in place. The right is the finished candle.

When the candle has cooled completely (I usually let them sit overnight) you can remove the end cap and top ring. Remove the duct tape and open the PVC pipe. Your candle is complete.

Moveable Candle Wicks

For many years I used the Nuwick 44 Hour Candle which had Moveable Wicks. The name of the candle was Trademarked and the moveable wicks were Patented and were pretty neat. You could put one, two, or three in the can containing the wax, depending on the amount of light or heat you wanted.

I was always interested in the moveable wicks, as they were unique. A few years ago I was looking at the wicks and something about them was very familiar, but I couldn't figure out what it was. Then one day I was making a leather sheath. I got out one of my pipe cleaners, as I use them to apply the edge dressing to my sheaths and holsters. Holding the pipe cleaner, I recognized it as the same type of material as the Nuwick moveable wicks. They had wire on the inside, and the outside were cotton. The only difference is they were not coated in wax.

Once the light went on in my head, I had to try to see if I could replicate the Nuwick moveable wick. As it turned out, I was correct and the wicks I made were just as functional as the Nuwick wicks.

The following is a quick photo tutorial on how you can make these moveable wicks for yourself. They work great in a can of paraffin or beeswax without wicks in them. You can use any old type container you want to use. I use an 8 oz. Screw Top Tin which are available at SurvivalResources.com.

Before I go any further, I did mention that these moveable wicks were Patented. I did a search and as far as I can tell, the

Patent ran out and was not renewed. Whether it is active or not, it is not illegal to replicate a patented item, it is only illegal to sell it. So making these wicks for yourself is not a problem.

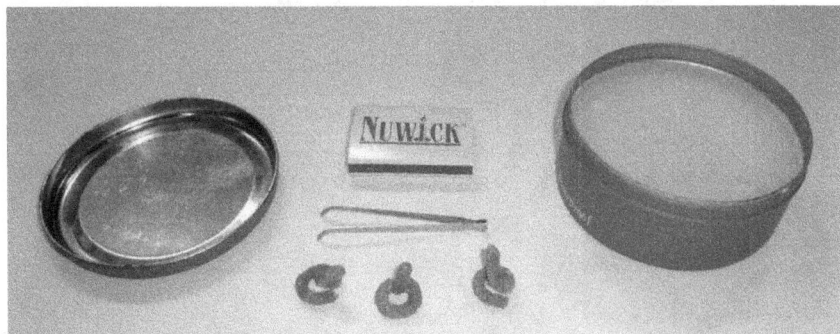

This the original Nuwick 44 Hour Candle with matches, tweezers, and 3 moveable wicks.

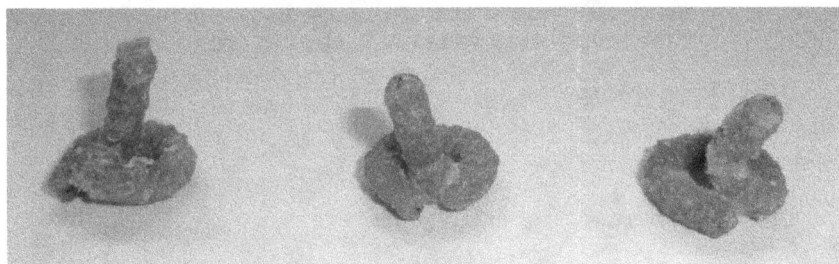

This is a close-up of the Nuwick Moveable Wicks.

Before you start there are a few supplies you will need in order to complete this project. First, and foremost, you will need some All Cotton pipe cleaners. You will need a pencil, or something of a similar diameter, and a pair of tweezers. For tools, I suggest a pair of side cutter pliers, and a pair of needle nose pliers. You will also need some melted paraffin or beeswax.

The first step is to twist a pipe cleaner into the shape of the Nuwick moveable wick. I do this by twisting it around a pencil until it meets itself, and then bend it in and then up. I leave approximately 1/2" standing up in the center, then cut off the remainder of the pipe cleaner with the side cutter pliers. I use the

needle nose pliers to shape the center piece to lean in and then up
needle nose pliers to shape the center piece to lean in and then up
in the middle. After doing several, you can normally shape it with
your fingers, after wrapping it around the pencil.

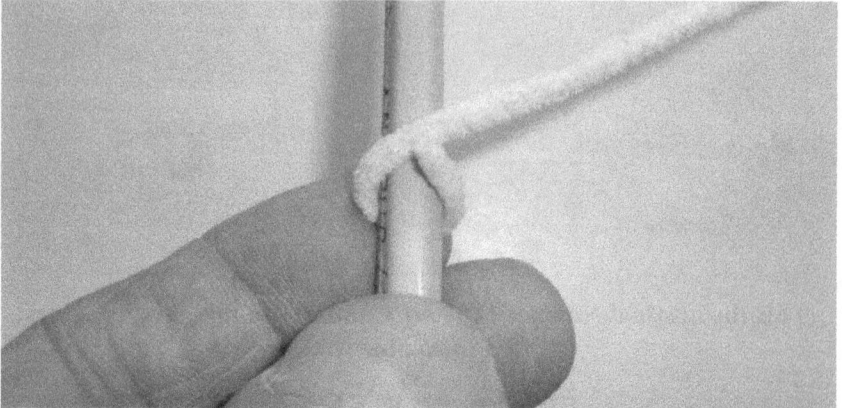

This shows the initial wrap of the pipe cleaner around the pencil.

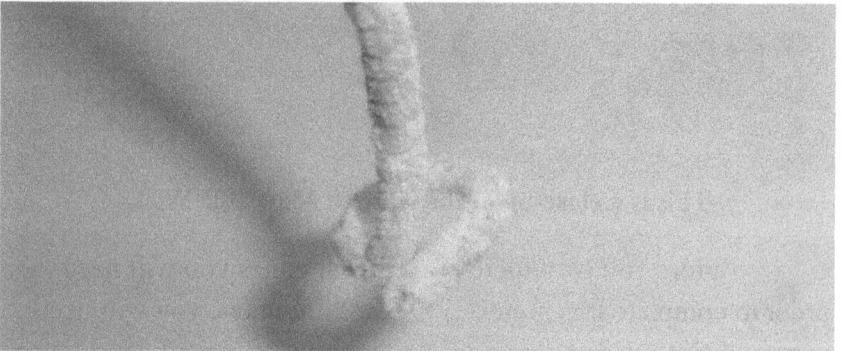

This shows the bending in and up of the remainder of the cotton pipe cleaner.

Three future moveable wicks after trimming the height.

Normally while I'm doing the above, I have the double boiler going on the stove so that the paraffin, or beeswax, is melted and ready for the dipping of the wicks to be. Once the wax is melted, I take each pipe cleaner wick and dip it in the liquid, using tweezers, and then set it on a piece of aluminum foil to harden. I do this with each of the pipe cleaner wicks. I then start over and dip each again, and back to the aluminum foil. I normally do this process four times, but you can do it as many times as you see fit. The idea is to build up a good coat of wax on the pipe cleaner wicks.

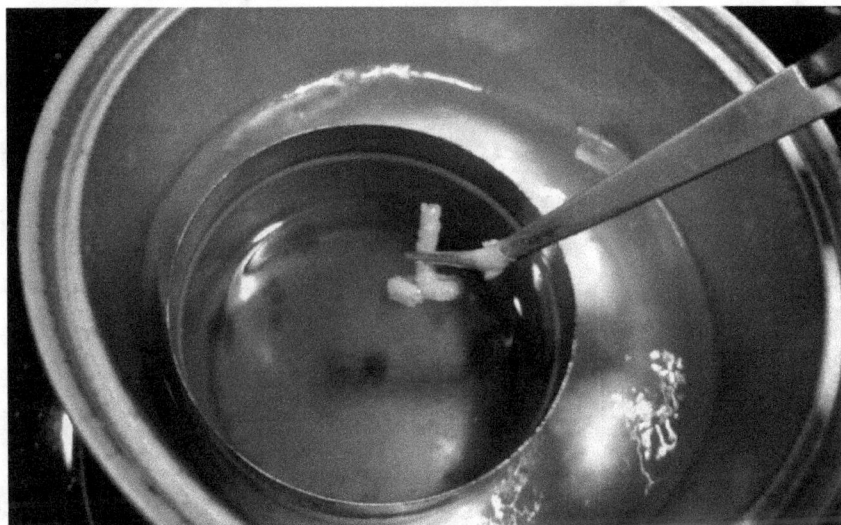

Dipping the pipe cleaner wick in the melted paraffin.

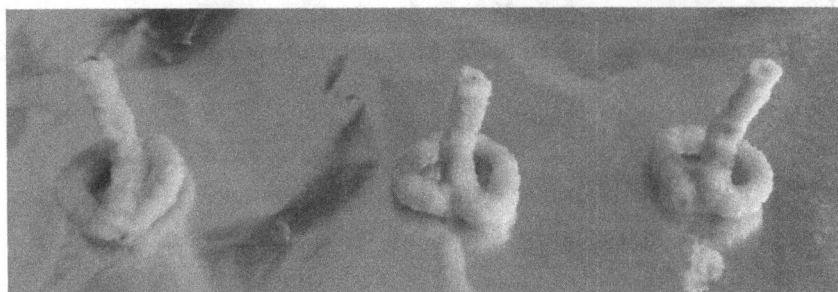

The completed moveable wicks after four coats of paraffin.

In order to use these moveable wicks, you will need to make a candle without a wick in some type of a container. Again, I use the 8 oz. screw top tin. You can use any type container and I have made some in an Altoids tin. The problem with a container that is not very tall is that you cannot store the wicks inside when not in use.

When you use the wicks, you just light them and set them on the wick-less candle. It will initially sit on top of the paraffin until it starts to melt the paraffin in the container. It will then make a small pool of liquid paraffin and it will sit there burning like a regular wick. You can use one, two, or as many as you need, or will fit, in your chosen container.

This shows three wicks being used and the pool of paraffin they float on.

When you are done using your candle, blow out the wicks and, using tweezers, remove them from the container and let them cool and harden. I usually set the hot wicks in the lid of the tin. Once the candle, and wicks have cooled, you can place the wicks in the container and they will be ready for the next use. They can be used over and over again.

This shows the wicks cooling in the lid as the candle cools.

As you can see, there are a lot of options for buying or making your own candles. There are various other ways to make your own candles , including dipping wicks and adding new coats as the previous dries. This is just a sampling, and I'm sure you can find other ideas on the internet.

Oil Lamps

Ever since I was a young boy, I remember having glass oil lamps at the house. They were kept on a shelf in the cellar, with a plastic bag over them to keep them clean. When the power went out, they were ready to go. I am fortunate that I inherited all of those lamps, and I have added to them over the years

Although you have to be careful with them, because they are glass, they are both useful and an attractive decoration. As you recall from Chapter 8 - Just In Case Supplies, we keep a good supply of lamp oil on hand.

There are many different styles and models of glass oil lamps available, but there are also various ways you can make your own lamps. Although we have lamp oil for our large lamps and lanterns (which we will discuss later in this chapter), you can use mineral oil, olive oil, Canola oil, etc. for homemade lamps.

This is a view of some of the author's oil lamps.

Mason Jar Adapter

If you like oil lamps, a handy item I have found is a Mason Jar Lamp Burner Adapter. This is basically an oil lamp burner that can be screwed directly to the top of a 2-3/4 inch diameter mason jar top. They are available from Oillampman.com and you can also buy the glass globes to fit it. Even though you can buy them in single packs, they have a four pack for only $13.50, which will give you four oil lamps from using four of your own mason jars. You can purchase the three inch glass chimneys from various sources.

You can also buy just an adapter ring that will allow you to use the screw on burner from an old oil lamp. This could come in

handy if you break a glass lamp. They are available from
Lehman's.com.

**This shows a Mason Jar Oil Lamp Burner Adapter which allows
you to turn any 2-3/4 inch diameter mason jar top into an oil lamp.**

Wine Bottle Oil Lamps

I found a commercially made wine bottle wick that has a
ceramic cork shaped stopper that has a hole in it for a wick to be
threaded through. You fill the bottle with oil and you have a wine
bottle lamp.

This shows a commercial wine bottle wick with a ceramic stopper.

Although the commercial unit certainly works, I felt it
would be just as easy to make something myself. I have some new

wine bottles that have metal screw caps. I took one of those and drilled a hole in the top to accommodate a one quarter inch grommet. I then placed the grommet through the hole in the screw cap and pressed it in place with a grommet setter. This keeps the hole from being sharp and possibly cutting the wick. I then threaded a long wick through the grommet and I had a wine bottle oil lamp. When using it, you just have to wait for it to cool before removing the metal screw cap.

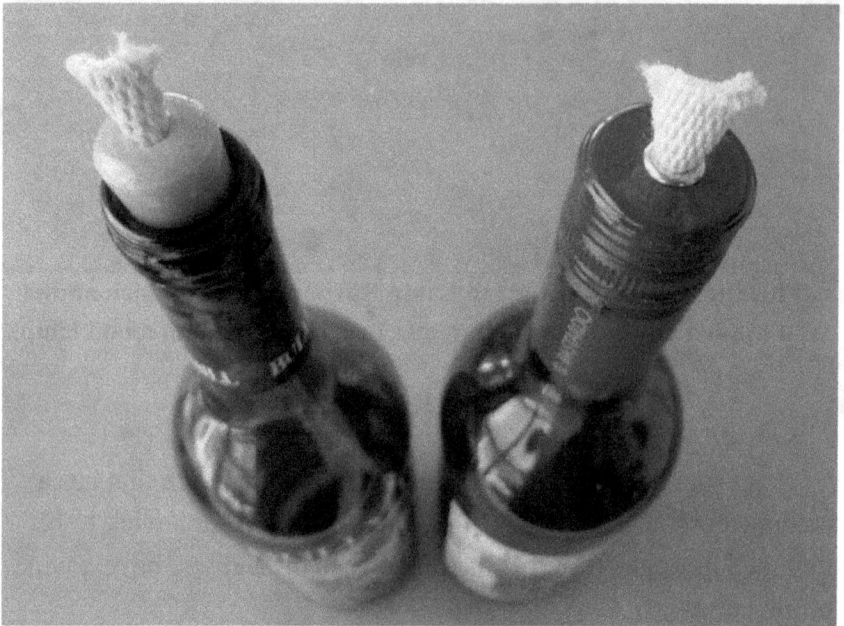

The wine bottle on the left shows the commercial ceramic bottle wick. The bottle on the right shows the author's homemade wick holder using a metal screw cap and a grommet.

Although the wine bottle lamps can be fun, I have found that without a globe to protect the flame, they can't be used in an area with any breeze. There are some globes available at the same commercial establishments that sell the ceramic stopper. I would suggest getting one.

Slush Lamps

Another type of oil lamp is called a "Slush Lamp" and is basically any type of small lamp where you float a wick, or in some manner hold a wick, in oil and use this as a lamp.

I have experimented with various configuration and the first one is using a cork to float a wick in a glass jar of oil. Instead of using a real wick, I usually just use a piece of jute cordage as the wick, and it works fine.

I take a real cork and cut off a slice. I then make a small hole in the center of the cork using a small awl on my pocket knife. In order to keep the cork from burning, I cut a small round piece of thin metal from a soda or beer can, the same diameter as the cork. I then make a small cut from the outside to the center, then cut a very small "V" at the center. I then bend the small "V" shaped pieces back.

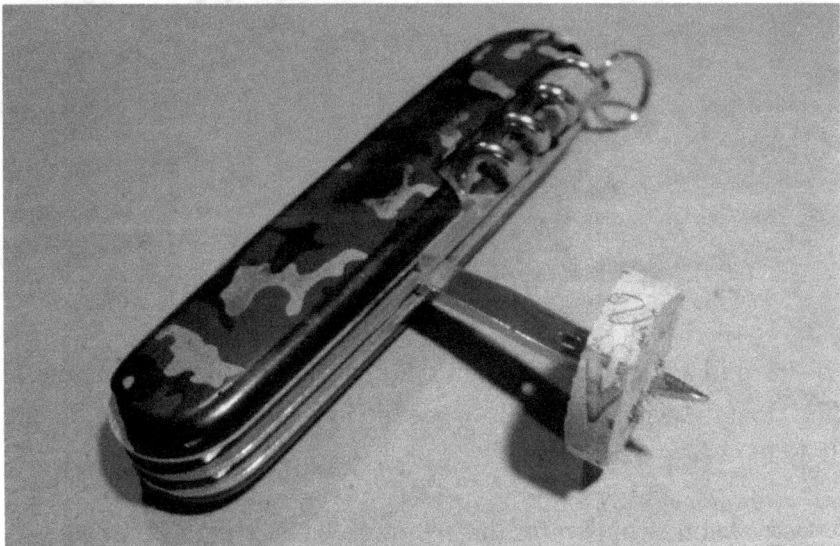

This shows using a small awl on a knife to make a small round hole in a slice of cork.

This shows the jute cordage, metal cap made from a can, and a slice of cork with a hole in it.

I now thread the Jute cordage through the hole. I then open the slit on the round piece of metal can and place it around the wick, on top of the cork.

This is a close-up view of the completed floatable wick.

Fill a small jar with lamp oil (or Olive oil, Canola oil, etc.) and float the wick in the oil. Once the jute soaks up the oil you can light it.

Another option for this, is to place water in the glass jar first, then oil on the top. When the wick burns up all the oil, it will put itself out once it hits the water.

A view of the floatable wick lamp using a shallow mason jar.

Under the "Moveable Candle Wicks" heading earlier in this chapter, I used Cotton Pipe Cleaners dipped in paraffin which would float on top of a candle, making them moveable.

One day, I was looking at the shape of the wicks made from the cotton pipe cleaners and I wondered if I dipped them in oil for a slush lamp, would they work as a "Free Standing" wick. Of course, you don't want them dipped in paraffin first. I just bent them in the same manner as for the moveable wicks.

I tried dipping them in both Olive Oil and Canola Oil and they worked great using either oil. Of course you can use lamp oil, or mineral oil, but I wanted to be able to use oil right out of the kitchen.

The size I used for the moveable wicks was perfect for a shallow dish, and I used a dish we use for Soy sauce. If you were going to use a deeper dish, you would just make the wicks taller.

This shows a slush lamp in a shallow dish using a cotton pipe cleaner as a wick.

Lanterns

For a great lighting fixture, I like to have lanterns as they are very durable, stable when sitting, and have a bail to hang them from. Most lanterns can burn standard lamp oil, kerosene, and synthetic kerosene.

For use in the house, I only use lamp oil as it less flammable (hence less dangerous) and produces much less unpleasant smelling fumes.

There are various manufacturers of lanterns on the market, but I personally prefer Dietz lanterns. The R.E. Dietz Company was started in 1940 and are best known for their hot blast and cold blast kerosene lanterns. They were always made in upper New York here in the U.S. However, in 1956, manufacturing was moved to Hong Kong, and then in 1982, manufacturing was moved to China.

I find the Dietz lantern to have the best quality of any of the lanterns I have used, and I now use them exclusively.

This is view of some of the Dietz Lanterns that the author has.

The left photo above shows how the author hangs a Dietz lantern between two windows in the dinette. The photo on the right shows a Dietz lantern that hangs from a chain over the author's kitchen sink. Both are ready when needed.

As you can see, there are various options for the self-reliant in regard to non-electrical lighting. In the next chapter we will discuss some electrical lighting options as well as alternative power sources.

Chapter 12
Alternative Power

There are different types of alternative power that can be utilized for self-reliance. Some are very simple, and others can get technical and complicated. I will offer various ideas that can be used by most people in various situations, depending on your location.

Simple Solar

I often hear people say that they wish they could take advantage of solar power, but it is just too expensive and elaborate to set up. I disagree, as all solar power does not consist of a large array of solar panels, battery controllers, and inverters. It can be very simple as a supplemental power source, or even as a way to reduce your requirement for electricity generated by the grid. You can use smaller systems to recharge batteries, cell phones, or other electrical devices.

The following is an example of thinking outside of the box. Many people have landscape lights that run on solar, but few people think about taking off the tops and using them in the house as supplemental lighting. We found that each top could be placed in a room for enough lighting to walk around. Just take the tops off with a twist and turn them upside down. Being the solar strip on top is now in the dark, the LED light comes on. We used them on our night stands at night.

One thing you might want to look for, is solar landscape lights that have a small slide switch to turn them off when you don't want them on, such as the ones we use on our night stands. When we go to bed, we can switch them off, and conserve the internal rechargeable batteries at the same time.

This is a typical landscaping LED Solar Light.

This photo shows the light given off by one of the small LED landscaping light heads. This was taken while it was light out, and it provides even more light in the dark.

Some of them don't have switches but you can easily modify them with a micro switch from an electronics store, like Radio Shack. I have opened the bottom and drilled a small hole, I then insert a small micro switch and connect it by cutting one of the wires to the battery and connecting one end to each terminal on the switch. It works like a charm. You can even get fancy and label the "On" and "Off", like I did, so you don't have to guess.

The left head has a small slide switch that allows you to switch the light on and off. The center head is one that the author modified with a small micro switch so it can also be turned on and of. The right photo shows a typical micro switch which was used to modify the center light.

This landscape light uses a standard AA rechargeable battery so you can use these lights to recharge AA rechargeable batteries.

It should also be noted that many of the battery compartments for landscaping lights hold AA Batteries. Not all do, but you can check before you purchase them. If they do, you can use them to recharge your AA rechargeable batteries. Just leave them in the yard during the day and your batteries will be recharging. You can then use them in an emergency for radios, head lamps, etc.

This is a view of an outdoor landscaping spotlight. The top shows the solar panel charging unit and below is the spotlight, modified with a hand clamp, for mounting in various locations.

Another useful solar device available for outdoor landscaping use is a solar spot light (shown in photo above). When I saw this I never planned on using it outside. I purchased it just for use inside the house. It is very useful because the solar charging panel is on a separate unit that can be left on a windowsill that normally faces the sun. The spotlight, which has a very bright LED, comes with 20 feet of wire and can be plugged into the solar charging panel unit. It normally comes with a mount that sticks into the ground and allows you to pivot the light up or down. I wanted to be able to clamp it to various things in the house and so I modified it by removing the ground stake and bolting a clamp to it. It can now be clamped to a window ledge, side of a bookcase, etc.

A view of the solar spotlight, discussed in the text, mounted over a windowsill to illuminate a room at night.

There are numerous small devices on the market that have a small solar panel attached and will keep those items running, as long as you have sun.

Another very handy portable solar device is called the LuminAid Solar-Powered Inflatable Light. This a great little solar device that folds very small and flat and can easily be kept on a south-facing window ledge to keep it charged. When you need it, you unfold it, blow it up, and you now have light to illuminate a room, or even carry around the house like a flashlight.

I am impressed with the amount of light the LuminAid gives off, and I even did a video review of it so you could see the actual illumination given off in the dark. If you would like to see that video it is posted under "Product Reviews" in the "Articles & Tips" section at SurvivalResources.com.

The LuminAid Solar Powered Inflatable Light is hand sized when folded up. Keep on a south facing window ledge to keep charged.

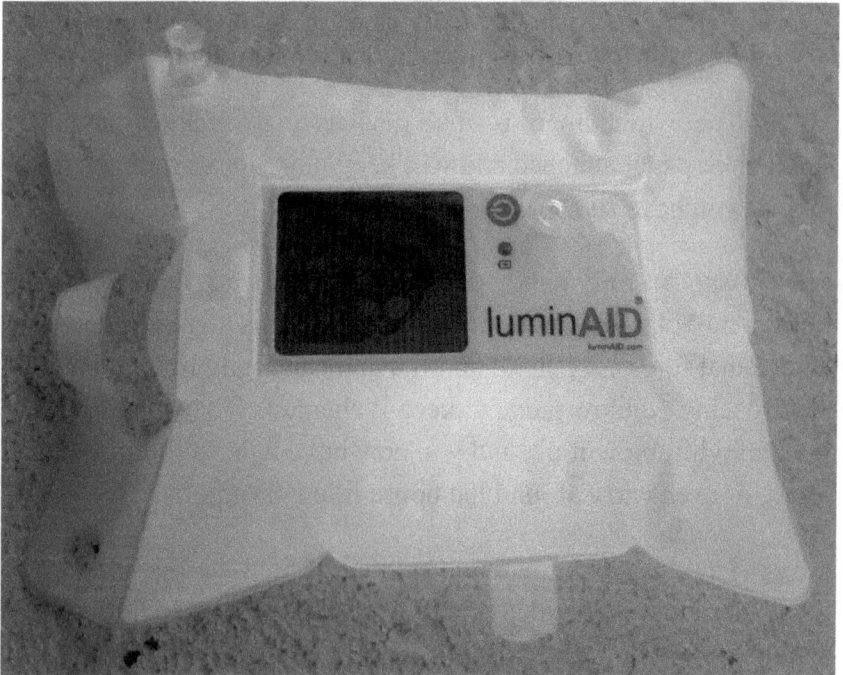

When unfolded and blown up, the LuminAid becomes a lantern that is waterproof and floats.

In order to keep the above discussed items charged, I placed a board in a south-facing window at an angle. I then placed the various items on the board, holding them in place with a small nail that sticks up and holds the item. This board stays in the window and when we need a light they are ready to go. When night comes we have free light without wasting batteries or oil in our lamps. If nothing else these devices can supplement what you use for lighting.

Various landscape lights, landscape spotlight solar panels, and two LuminAids that stay in this south-facing window, on a board mounted at a slant on the inside.

In order to recharge our cell phones, IPad, IPod, Kindles and spare rechargeable batteries we use various products from GoalZero. For batteries and cell phones, we use the Guide 10 Plus Solar Kit which allows us to charge either AA or AAA batteries (which can be used for battery operated devices like a headlamp, radios, etc) and our cell phones either using an included solar panel, or with AC using a USB cable. With the batteries in the device, it is also a flashlight with a built-in LED, and will also power two optional lights that plug into it. A really handy and versatile device.

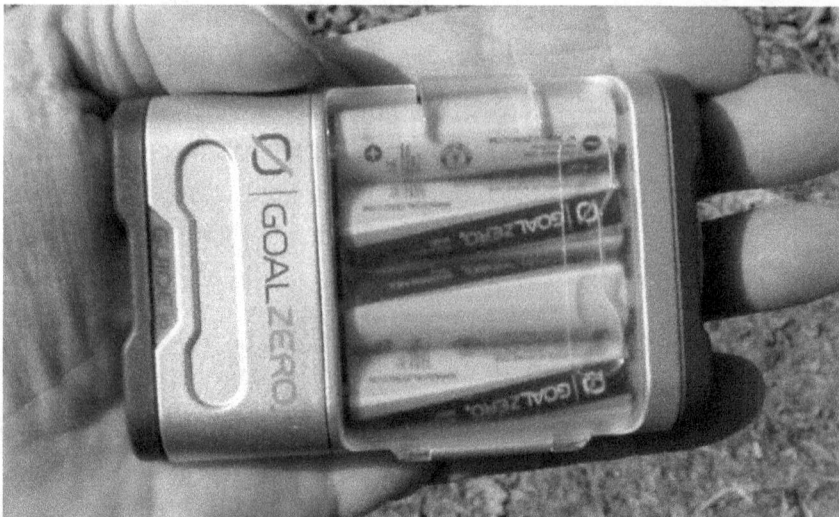

The Guide 10 Plus Recharger is small enough to fit in your hand.

This is a view of the Guide 10 Plus with the Nomad 7 Solar Panel, both made by GoalZero.

The Nomad 7 is an ultra-compact solar panel that enables you to charge The Guide 10 Plus Recharger, or your handheld devices directly from its USB and 12 Volt DC charging ports. It collects 7 Watts of power from the sun. It is a foldable, rugged design, and weather resistant. The Nomad 7 will directly charge most USB and 12V devices (not tablets), most handheld USB devices, including: cell phones, smart phones, GPS's, and MP3 players. The Nomad 7 Solar Panel can be chained together with other panels for increased collection.

Another GoalZero product I like is the Sherpa 50 Recharger Solar Recharging Kit. It is an ultra-portable power supply to keep laptops and tablets, and other electronic devices charged. Being it has a 12V output as well as a 5V USB output, you can even use it to run a 12V television panel, as well as other 12V devices. It also has a 19V laptop output with charging cable. We purchased several of these units with the Sherpa 13 solar panels and a couple with the AC inverter.

The Sherpa 50's come in real handy when the power goes out and we also use them when we are in the field. We keep the Sherpa 50's plugged into AC power all the time which is an advantage with these units. They have built in charge controllers so you don't have to unplug them when they are fully charged.

When the power goes out, they are ready to go, and you can recharge them using the Sherpa 13 solar panel.

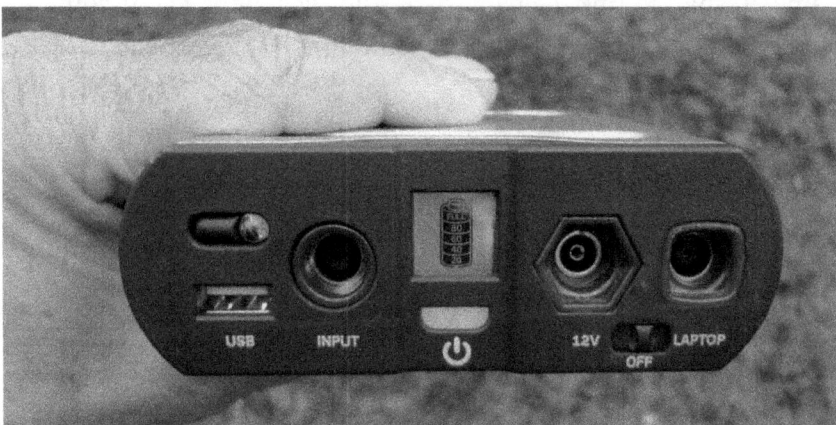

The Sherpa 50 being hand held to show the size of the unit.

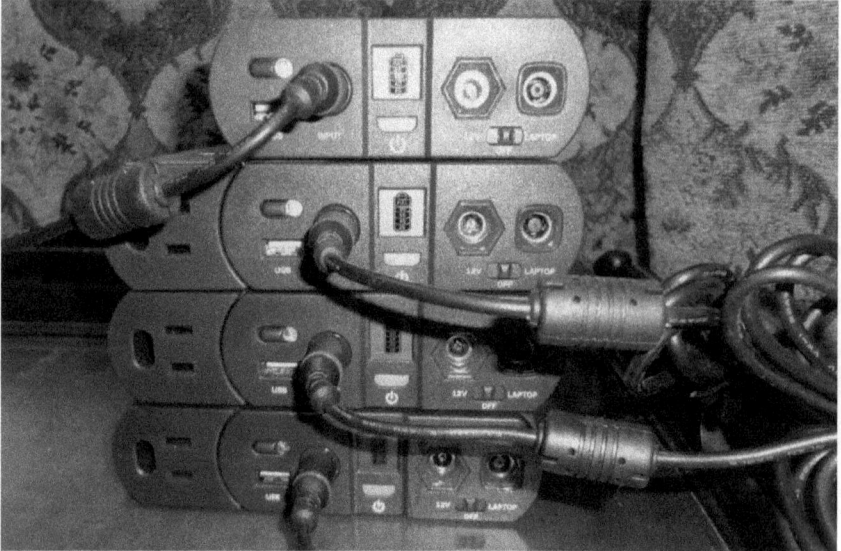

The author's Sherpa 50's remain plugged in on a small table so they are ready when he needs them.

Another feature I like about the GoalZero solar panels is that they are all chainable. This means that you can link various sized solar panels together to increase the amount of charging ability you have going to the GoalZero rechargers, or you can actually recharge 12 volt batteries with them. They all have a 12 volt output and you can mix different sizes, as they all function the same. Cables to link the panels are sold separately, and if you purchase more than one panel, I would highly suggest you get a linking cable.

I have various sized portable panels for various needs. They are foldable, so they are convenient for storage. When the power goes out, I have hooks that I made from coat hanger wire for one south facing window, and I can hang one of the larger panels in the window for charging various devices. It is not optimum as the panel hangs flat, and is not angled to the sun, but it does collect power. However, when it is a nice sunny day, I just lay them out on the lawn and angle them the best I can.

This shows various sized portable and foldable solar panels that the author uses for various recharging requirements.

This shows a larger portable solar panel hanging on the inside of a south facing window when the power goes out. It can recharge various devices, or recharge batteries.

This is a closer view of the hooks the author made from coat hanger wire in order to hang the portable solar panel in front of a south facing window.

A view of the potable solar panel hung in a window, from outside.

Another simple item that many people don't think of is a solar powered radio. Many of these are hand held, and can be powered by the sun. We have various sized radios and one sits on our screened in porch and is charged daily from the sun. We use it around the yard and in the garden. It is free power and we use it whenever we can.

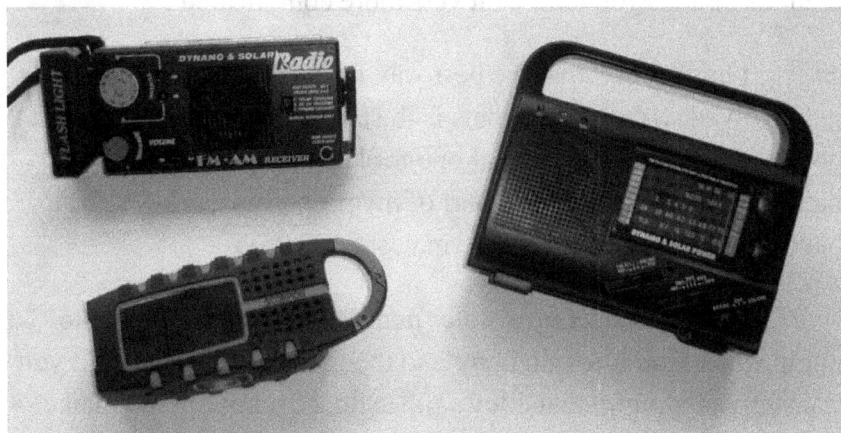

All three of the above radios have small solar panels on them and are charged by the sun.

As you can see, using the power of the sun for solar devices does not have to be complicated. However, larger and more sophisticated solar systems can produce more power and provide you with an alternate source of energy.

Photovoltaic Solar Systems

In this section I will discuss photovoltaic solar systems (also called PV Systems). Simply put, solar radiation is converted into direct current electricity. We saw this in the previous heading, "Simple Solar". I will not provide detailed information in regard to actually hooking up the systems, as that is beyond the scope of this book. There are many books and other sources available on understanding Photovoltaic's and designing systems.

It should be noted that larger systems can be dangerous. The energy may be coming from the sun, but the power generated can shock, or kill, if systems are not grounded, or properly installed. You will also get involved with mounting panels, charge controllers for a battery system, and AC inverters to provide you with 110 volt alternating current. Of course, there is more to it than this, but as you can see it gets more complicated

I have found that the best way for the self-reliant person to get involved with solar systems is to start small. The first system I got involved with was a small one for keeping a 50 Ah, 12 volt battery, charged in the back part of my property where we don't have electricity. The solar system cost $139.95.

I wanted to set up a water pump that would allow me to pump water from the rain barrels to the garden. I located a 12 volt transfer water pump that allows me to attach a hose to the intake and stick that hose in a water barrel. A hose is then attached to the output of the pump and this hose can be run to the garden. When the pump is running, it draws water out of the barrels and delivers it to the garden where we can water the plants. It really beats the multiple trips we need to take carrying buckets of water.

This is a simple system that we purchased ready to go. It has a simple frame (that needs to be assembled) and four 15 Watt panels attach to the frame, providing us with 60 watts at 12 volts. The system came with a charge controller, which keeps the battery charged, but doesn't allow it to overcharge. It also came with an AC inverter, which provides alternating current, but we don't use it. However, it is available should we need to run a power tool or lights back in that area. It should also be noted, that this entire system can be easily moved down by the house, or elsewhere if needed.

The solar panels simply sit on the ground by the potting shed, at an angle, provided by legs at the rear of the frame. The wires run from the panels, inside the potting shed, where the charge controller and 50 Ah (amp hour) battery is situated. The solar panels keep the battery charged at all times, and when I need to use the transfer water pump, I connect it to the battery using large electrical alligator clips at the end of a roll of wire which is permanently attached to the pump. When I'm done watering, the wire is disconnected from the battery and the pump and wires are stored in the potting shed.

This is the charge controller, mounted on the wall, and the 50 Ah battery in the author's potting shed. It is kept charged with the 60 Watt solar panels outside of the shed.

This is the 60 Watt solar panel that simply sits on the ground near the author's potting shed, which keeps a 50 Ah battery charged, and ready to power the 12 volt water pump.

The transfer water pump is a self-priming, and was designed for the transfer of liquids in commercial and industrial applications. It cannot be submerged so it sets on the ground between the potting shed and garden. I purchased it from Northern Tool and Equipment for $49.99, which was more than reasonable for a piece of equipment that makes the watering the garden much less of a chore.

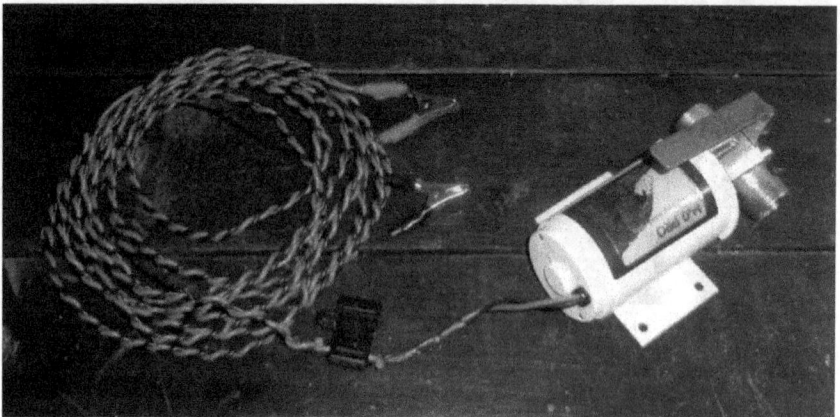

A view of the 12 volt water transfer pump with wires and electrical alligator clips attached.

Solar systems can grow from this simple type, to systems that can essentially provide power for all your needs, and anything in between. Of course it depends on various factors such as, what your needs are, how elaborate you need the system to be, how much exposure you have to the sun, and how much you want to spend.

If a photovoltaic solar system is being designed for self-reliance, keep the following in mind. I know of several people who have spent a lot of money (50 to 70 thousand dollars) for a photovoltaic solar system that is tied to the grid. They produce electricity from their solar panels, but this is fed into the grid whereby they are credited for this power and their power bill is reduced.

I was talking to one of these individuals and asked what type of battery storage he had. He said he didn't have any battery storage and all the electricity produced was fed to the grid. I asked him what happens when the power goes out. He said, "Then we don't have any electricity."

Well, maybe it is just my opinion, and being self-reliant, but if I spent thousands on a photovoltaic solar system, and the power went out, I would like to have electricity. As you can see, some people have a system for the purpose of reducing their power bill, not for the purpose of self-reliance. I feel if you are going to spend the money to have a system, then at least collect some of that electricity, and store it in batteries, so it can be used when the power goes out.

You should also note that a grid-tie system is much more complicated than an off-grid system, so you will need to have a professional install it in most cases, unless you are very savvy with solar installation and electrical regulations as the system must meet code in order to connect to the grid.

For the above reason, I prefer an Off-Grid photovoltaic solar system. Again, it can be as large or small as your needs require. You can have a 12-volt or 24-volt system, and if your panels are further than fifty feet from your batteries and charge controller, you will probably have to go 24-volt. As my friend, Steve Gregersen, explains in his book, "Creating the Low Budget Homestead," he prefers a 12-volt system because it is less expensive, because in a 24-volt system, you need to buy components, such as panels and batteries, in doubles.

My good friends, Steven and Susan Gregersen, provide all their own electricity on their homestead in Montana, with an off-grid photovoltaic solar system that they designed and built themselves. The frame for the solar panels was built using salvaged pipe, old bed rails, and a welder. It started with five panels, and more recently, they have added another two panels at top. It provides for all of their electrical needs.

This is the front view of the solar panel array built by Steve Gregersen out of salvaged pipe and old bed rails. It provides for all of his Off-Grid electrical needs. Photo by Steve Gregersen

This is a rear view of the Gregersen's solar array showing the homemade frame and the wiring. It can be swiveled to follow the sun, or adjusted for seasonal angle. Photo by Steve Gregersen

I have only touched on the very basics of photovoltaic solar systems. There is a lot more to understand in regard to, determining your electrical needs in watts, and then designing and building a system to meet those needs. However, as a supplement to your normal electrical power from the grid, you can start small and add as you go., This will allow you to reduce your dependency on the grid.

Human Power

Something I often find missing in books on alternative energy or power is the advantage of "Human Power." What I mean by this, is the use of equipment or machinery that get their power from human power, such as pedal operated or hand-crank operated devices.

We already covered two devices in Chapter-7. One was the foot powered sewing machine. It is operated by moving the foot up and down on a hinged foot plate. My wife has a spinning wheel for making yarn, and this is operated by foot power, utilizing a hinged foot plate. Another device I mentioned in Chapter-7 was the bicycle attachment for our grain mill. You utilize a bicycle to operate the grain-mill, by pedaling the bike, which through a pulley belt system, turns the drive wheel of the grain mill. I have also seen an ancient lathe that was run by foot power and it would still be effective today. You are essentially using human energy to provide mechanical energy.

But not all of these devices need to be mechanical. There are various electrical devices, such as radios, that have a fold-out crank handle which essentially allows you to crank an alternator which produces electrical energy to run the device, and in some cases, recharge the batteries. As long as you have energy yourself, you can operate the device.

There are many more devices out there that can utilize human power to produce electrical power. I have seen various pedal power mechanisms that will produce power through a generator and then store it in a battery for later use.

The above photo shows the author's wife's spinning wheel which is operated by foot power.

It should be noted that in the picture under "Simple Solar" in the beginning of this chapter, the one that shows three solar powered radios, the two radios on the left have crank handles as well as the solar panels. I also have a large lantern type flashlight and regular lantern that is crank operated.

The photo above shows two of the author's crank lanterns. The one on the left is a lantern that collapses down when not in use. The one on the right also has a built-in radio.

These are just some examples of how "Human Power" can be used to reduce your reliance on other energy sources. Keep in mind, that many years ago, this WAS the only source of power.

Wind Power

When people think of wind power today they envision large turbines with huge blades sitting atop tall metal poles. Indeed that is modern wind power generating electrical power, but the concept isn't new.

Wind has been used as an energy source for a long time. Over 4,000 years ago the Babylonians and Chinese were pumping water for irrigating their crops using wind power. And even before that, sailing boats were using the wind for power. In Europe, in the Middle Ages, wind power was used to grind corn, and this is where the term "Windmill" came from.

As you can see, wind power is not just for generating electricity. Windmills are still used today for pumping water from wells.

This photo shows an old water pump windmill in Oklahoma. Water pump windmills are still being used today for farms and ranches, as well as domestic water supplies. Photo by Shane Link

There is a company in San Angelo, Texas called Aermotor Windmill Co. who has been making windmills since 1888. They manufacture windmills for pumping water and they are made here in the USA and distributed worldwide. They can be contacted at www.aermotorwindmill.com.

In some countries, both the older windmills, for pumping water, and the newer, electricity generating turbines, can be seen working together. But it is becoming very rare and those used to generate electricity are taking over.

Here is a great photo of a modern and traditional windmill on the countryside of Holland, close to the Hague. Photo by Erik Ferkranus

Of course, for a windmill or wind generator to work for you, you obviously need wind. You also need to get above any obstructions in order to capture the wind. This could require a large tower which usually involves zoning regulations, and if the turbine generates any undo noise, it can create a problem with neighbors. Even without the technical problems of installing a wind turbine, you can see you will first need to do your homework.

There are some smaller wind generators that are being designed and manufactured, and I have even seen one that can mount to a mast on the back of a motor home. The technical aspects of buying, or installing, wind generators for the purpose of generating electricity is beyond the scope of this book. However, there is plenty of information available if you are interested in this type of alternative power.

This shows a small wind turbine mounted above the peak of a house. Keep in mind that the turbine has to be higher than surrounding obstructions in order to capture the wind.

Water Power

Water Power, also called Hydro-power, is power which is derived from the energy of falling or running water. This power can be harnessed in order to run machinery, or to generate electricity power. Like wind power, which needs wind, water power needs falling or running water.

Water Wheels

A good example of this concept are water wheels. They have been used since ancient times to irrigate fields and run machinery. in some cases, water is diverted so that it runs over a water wheel, whereby the running water causes the wheel to turn, creating the power. However, in some cases, the running water is diverted so that it will then fall over the water wheel, whereby the falling water, is creating the power.

You would be surprise at the amount of energy that a simple water wheel can generate. While at the Living Museum at Ballenberg, Switzerland, which I have mentioned previously in this book, I was able to observe a waterwheel in actual operation running machinery.

At this location, they don't have a fast moving stream or other body of water. they utilize water, from several natural springs, which is diverted downhill to a large gutter like trough, called a "Flume." This collected water continues down the flume at a descending angle, gaining strength. The end of the flume is closed, so when the water meets the end, it is diverted downward through a chute, directly over a water wheel.

The large water wheel, which is connected to a large barn like structure, turns an axle. The length of this axle is the width of the lower barn area, and provides various options for belt powered machinery. Upstairs there is a large sawmill, completely operated by this water powered wheel, and it cuts huge lengths of wood into boards. The power derived from this wheel also runs a large oil press and a wheat grinder.

All of these operations are mechanical, and no electrical energy is produced, but it shows the amount of mechanical power that can be derived from the energy of running and falling water.

This shows the flume, at Ballenberg, Switzerland, directing the water from springs towards the water wheel.

This shows the water wheel, at Ballenberg, Switzerland, with water falling through the shoot from the flume above.

The sawmill was a huge area where complete logs were moved towards a large stationary band saw blade, where they were first squared, and then cut into boards. The complete operation was performed by two men, one running the saw, and one adjusting a rail type carrier that moved the wood into the saw blade. It was rather amazing to see how much power could be generated by diverted water.

This is a view of the sawmill operation at Ballenberg, Switzerland.

I'm sure at this point, you are wondering why I am discussing a water wheel in Switzerland. It is because it shows that being self-reliant doesn't require modern machinery or electricity. It also shows that if you have a source of running water, it can be utilized for self reliance.

Generating Electricity From Hydro-Power

Since the early 20th century we have been generating electricity through hydro-power. Many will envision a place like Hoover Dam, where electric power is generated for several states.

But the ability to generate electric power from hydro-power is also available to you with commercially manufactured, or home built units. Although there is a lot of information on the internet in regard to building your own, including videos, I have not attempted this as I do not have any running water on my property. Of course, if I did, I would be trying it out.

There are some large hydro-power units available that can provide both DC (direct) current, as well as AC (alternating) current. You will need some running water in order to use these type of units.

There is a nice unit manufactured by Lo Power Engineering which is called the Harris Hydroelectric Permanent Magnet Turbine. The Harris system is an efficient, durable battery-charging Pelton turbine.

This is a close-up view of the Harris Hydroelectric System manufactured by Low Power Engineering.
Photo courtesy of Lo Power Engineering

It is designed to produce usable household power from springs and creeks that are too small to sustain the same level of useful power from a conventional A.C. generating system.

Because D.C. can be stored (and A.C. cannot), the system is collecting power 24 hours a day, a little at a time, and stored in a battery, to be used as needed. An A.C. inverter can be run off the battery system for alternating current.

This is a view of the Harris Hydroelectric System installed at a location showing four water inputs.
Photo courtesy of Lo Power Engineering

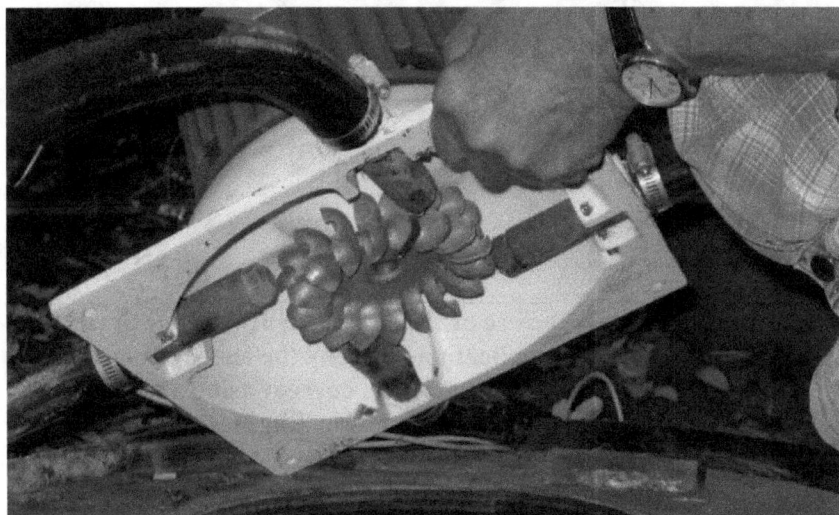

This is a view of the underside of the Harris Hydroelectric System showing the Pelton Type Runner and the four nozzle arrangement.
Photo courtesy of Lo Power Engineering

Off-Grid - DC Direct

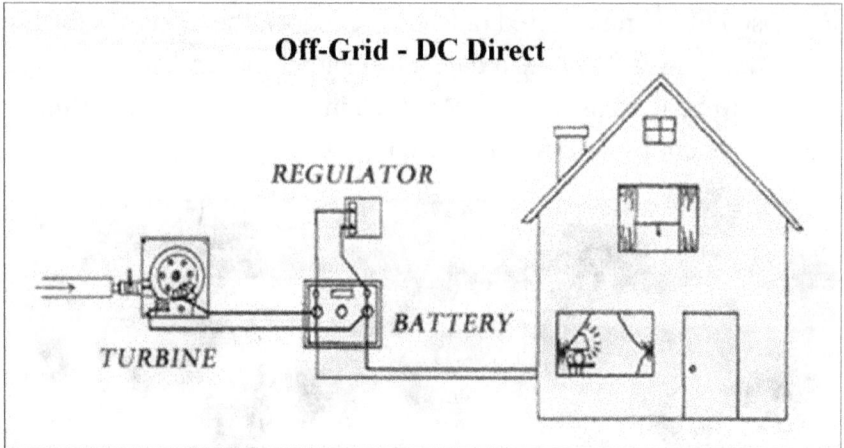

REGULATOR

BATTERY

TURBINE

This diagram shows the use of the Harris Hydroelectric System in an Off-Grid application whereby the energy is stored in batteries.
Diagram courtesy of Lo Power Engineering

Conventional House - 110 volt

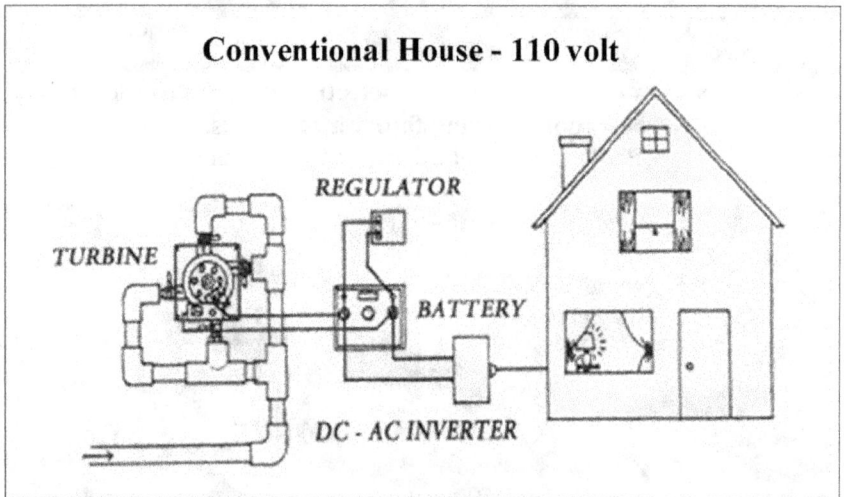

REGULATOR

TURBINE

BATTERY

DC - AC INVERTER

This diagram shows the use of the Harris Hydroelectric System in a conventional house application whereby the energy is stored in batteries, then used to generate A.C. current using an inverter.
Diagram courtesy of Lo Power Engineering

If you would like more information on the Harris Hydro-Electric System, they can be contacted at www.harrismicrohydro.com.

A company in Canada, called Energy Systems & Design, Ltd. makes various micro hydro power machines. They make one called the "Water Buddy" which is very small. This little machine generates DC power from a source such a stream running down a hillside, and provides many possibilities for charging batteries, pond lights, or even camping.

This is a view of the "Water Buddy," a small hydro power machine manufactured by Energy Systems Design Ltd. It is truly portable and can be used for various applications, including temporary installations such as camping.
Photo courtesy of Energy Systems & Design Ltd.

Some water is channeled into a pipeline that is long enough to build up sufficient pressure. It can also be used with water systems that are under pressure like the water in city supplies. The water then passes through a small nozzle where it gives up pressure for velocity. The water then passes through the turbine runner which converts the energy in the water into shaft power and spins the generator. In the generator there are magnets that move past coils of wire where the electricity is generated. This electric power is first alternating current (AC) that is converted into direct current (DC) with a device called a rectifier. The power then goes to the output terminals (binding posts) where it is available to charge batteries or use directly with suitable appliances.

The "Water Buddy" is only 6 inches square by 8 inches tall and provides 12/24 volts with up to 200 watts. They also have a 48/120 volt version.

I like this unit as you could package it as a kit, with some flexible tubing and a battery pack, and use it where you are. If you are camping and have a running stream, you could essentially have the means to recharge batteries or run some LED lighting. Something I might have to set-up.

They also have a larger unit called the "Stream Engine" and this unit employs a brushless, permanent magnet alternator which is adjustable, enabling the user to match turbine output to the electrical load. It has higher efficiency than previous alternators, and is capable of outputs up to 1+ kilowatt (kW).It is equipped with a rugged bronze turgo wheel, universal nozzles (adaptable to sizing from 3 mm (1/8 inch) to 25 mm (1 inch), or brass nozzle inserts, and a digital multimeter which is used to measure output current. The entire system is made of non-corrosive alloys for long life and durability.

Typically, these systems operate at 12, 24, or 48 volts, with re-connectable wiring which allows the user to install a standard turbine at most sites. Custom windings are also available which can produce high voltage (120, 240) at any site.

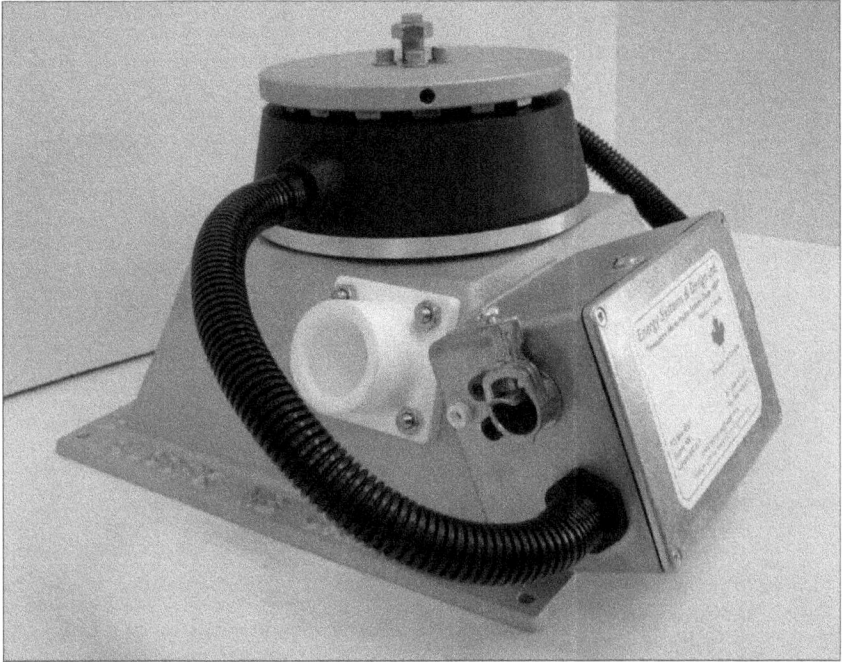

This is a view of the "Stream Engine," a larger hydro power machine manufactured by Energy Systems & Design Ltd.
Photo courtesy of Energy Systems & Design, Ltd.

If you have further interest in either the "Water Buddy" or the "Stream Engine" Energy Systems & Design, Ltd. can be contacted at www.microhydropower.com.

As you can see, the use of running or falling water certainly provides options for the self-reliant to power machinery or produce electricity. If you have flowing water on your property, you might want to examine this option further.

Chapter 13
<u>Sanitation & Hygiene</u>

Sanitation and Hygiene is an important element of staying healthy and self-reliant. Most people today rely on their toilet always working, the use of a washer and dryer to clean their clothes, and cleaning supplies always being available at their local store. Let's take a look at some options which can make us less dependent on others.

Toilets & Alternatives

Although not often discussed, if you eat you, will eventually have to dispose of the results of that food working its way through your system. That is where a toilet comes in handy.

Most people rely on a normal, conventional, toilet for this function. Unfortunately, your reliance on such a device normally also relies on having water to flush it. When the power goes out, after your first flush, water will not be pumped back into the tank that sits behind the throne. Most sewers will still function normally, but without water to flush your business down the pipes to the sewer, many people consider the toilet unusable until the water comes back on.

Of course this is a fallacy, as long as you have access to some water. This does not need to be potable water, as it can be water collected by various means, as discussed in Chapter 10.

There are two ways you can flush a toilet with a bucket of water. The first is to dump a bucket directly into the bowl. Dump the water slowly, but at a steady pace. If you dump it too slow, you will not get a complete flush, and you might have to do it again. Dump it too fast and you could get splashed, which you probably wouldn't desire. Therefore, I do it the second way, which is refilling the tank behind the throne itself.

This shows the author pouring water from a two gallon bucket into the water tank at the rear of the toilet in order to flush it when the power is out. Photo by Denise McCann

All you need to do, is remove the cover on the water tank at the back of the toilet. When you have completed your business, pour a gallon or two of water into the tank, and flush normally.

This allows the toilet to flush as it normally would, and you don't have to become the expert at dumping water at a specific pace.

I have a generator that will keep most things running normal when the power goes out. But if it is good weather, I won't bother wasting gas for the purpose of flushing a toilet. Instead, we use water from our rain barrels. We keep a two gallon bucket filled and stored in the bathroom. Whoever uses it goes out to the rain barrel and refills it.

If you live in the city or suburbs and don't have access to water for flushing when the power goes out, you might want to have an alternative means to dispose of your business. There are various portable toilets that can be used for short term situations. The following two are options that be handy to keep on hand just in case.

The first is called The Luggable Loo® Seat & Cover. It simply snaps onto, and allows you to turn, any five gallon spackle or paint bucket into a toilet.

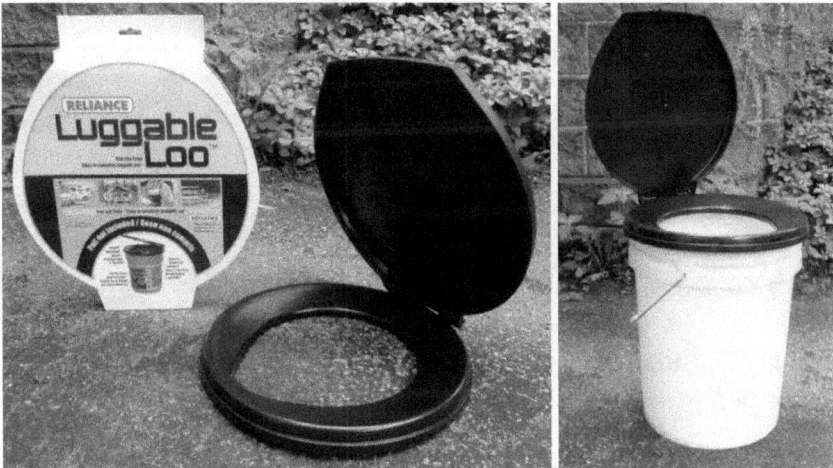

The left photo above shows the Luggable Loo lid and cover. The right photo shows it snapped onto a five gallon bucket for use as a toilet for a short term situation if you can't use your real toilet.

The Luggable Loo® Seat & Cover is a handy item as it is very flat, being only a lid, and stores very easily. When needed, grab one of your extra five gallon buckets, and you have a toilet. You can line the bucket with a plastic bag for later disposal, or you can also purchase Double Doodie Toilet Bags with Bio-Gel. These bags turn liquid waste into a solid gel. They are a sealable, leak-proof outer bag, that is sealed to an inner waste bag containing a Bio-Gel waste gelatin.

Another unit that is a little more comfortable to use is called the Fold-To-Go Collapsible Toilet. This unit takes more space for storage, but provides a more normal sitting configuration.

The left photo above shows the Fold-To-Go portable toilet in the folded position for storage. The right photo shows it in the open position with a Double Doodie Toilet Bag with Bio-Gel attached.

This collapsible portable toilet folds down to just 5 inches and weighs only 5 pounds. It has an integrated handle, making it easy to carry. It also boasts an innovative leg locking system, making it one of the sturdiest portable toilets around. Again, I would suggest Double Doodie Toilet Bags with Bio-Gel, which were originally designed for this toilet. Both the Luggable Loo® Seat & Cover and Fold-To-Go Collapsible Toilet are available from www.SurvivalResources.com.

If you are in the suburbs or the country, you will have more options for a toilet for the purpose of self-reliance. You can make your own toilet from a five gallon bucket and use some sawdust after each use, to cover your business. Keep a lid on the bucket until almost filled. Then take the bucket and empty it in a separate compost bin to let it continue composting (It should be noted that you should not use this compost in an edible garden, but you can use it for ornamental trees and shrubs

Using the sawdust type toilet concept, you can do the same thing outside, using the "outhouse" design. A small structure with a seat that is mounted over the bucket, or in this case, even a larger barrel. The procedure is the same. At the survival school where we used to teach wilderness survival, we had an outhouse that served all students for three seasons. We would then dump the barrel at another location on the property. It was quite the compost pile!

Another way to make a composting toilet is to use worms - yes worms. Let me relate a story from my good friend, Christopher Nyerges, from his book "Extreme Simplicity - Homesteading In The City."

Christopher, always experimenting with self-reliant ideas, conducted a test in his backyard. "In a secluded spot, he set up an outdoor toilet, which consisted of the toilet seat from a hospital-style potty and, instead of the usual pot under the seat, a large wooden box was used. This box was sized to fit under the toilet seat. Into the box he placed a layer of worms and worm castings and some partially decomposed straw. After each use of this toilet, the excrement was covered with another layer of worms and worm castings. This system proved to be simple, odor-free, and fly-free. The key to its success was the addition of the earthworms. Christopher used the type of earthworms known as red-worms, which are the most common variety bred in backyard worm farms because they are rapid breeders and can tolerate broad fluctuations in temperature. Earthworms are great partners in the composting process: they continually burrow and digest organic matter, breaking it down into nitrogen-rich plant food.

After the box under the toilet became full, it was moved to the side to give the earthworms time to process the contents, and the toilet seat was placed on top of another wooden box. Two months was adequate for the full decomposition of all excrement and toilet paper in a box. The contents of each seasoned box - a rich, loamy soil full of earthworms - were distributed around the base of fruit trees".

This illustrates that sometimes experimentation can resolve an issue, or at least provide you with other options. Christopher has spent years examining various ways to be self-reliant and continues in that endeavor today.

Commercial Composting Toilets

A commercial composting toilet must perform three completely separate processes. First, it must compost the waste and toilet paper quickly and without odor. Second, it must ensure that the finished compost is safe and easy to handle. And third, it must evaporate the liquid.

There are various manufacturers that make self-contained units. However, most small, self-contained composting toilets are really designed for the seasonal or cabin type use, and are not designed to handle, full-time, daily use. Some of the manufactures that are best known for these type of units include Sun-Mar and Envirolet. They both make composting toilets that can be used inside the home, and Sun-Mar makes some larger scale units that can be centralized, whereby the toilet is in the bathroom and the composter is below, such as a cellar. These units are for full-time residential use.

Another option was introduced by a man named Joseph Jenkins. He is the author of the book, " The Humanure Handbook - A Guide to Composting Human Manure, 3rd edition," which has sold over 55,000 copies. Although there are many books available on manure and how to use it, this is the first book on human manure composting. It is a comprehensive book on recycling human excrement without chemicals, high technology, or pollution.

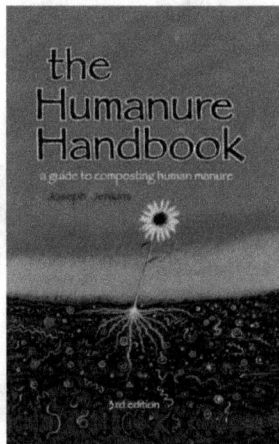

This is the cover of "The Humanure Handbook" written by Joseph Jenkins, a comprehensive book on recycling human excrement without chemicals, high technology, or pollution.

When Joseph Jenkins wrote the "The Humanure Handbook" and thereby introduced the world to the "humanure toilet," he didn't expect people to write to him saying they loved their little compost toilets, but many did. A lot of them built their own toilets from instructions in the book.

In time, people started asking Jenkins to provide them with these little toilets, already constructed. They wanted them for their homes, camps, cabins, cottages, and to keep in a basement corner for emergency use should the power go out. So he set-up shop and started making them. The finished toilet, called the "Loveable Loo Eco Toilet" is approximately 18" wide, 21" long and a little higher than the toilet receptacle, approximately 17".

This is the basic "Loveable Loo Eco Toilet" made by the author of "The Humanure Handbook" and sold at the Humanure Store.
Photo courtesy of Joseph Jenkins, Inc.

Basically this toilet is a plywood box with a hinged top that allows you to place a five gallon bucket (four five gallon buckets with lids are included) inside, whereby it is held in place with a round hole cut in the hinged top. On top of this is a hinged toilet seat with cover. You also receive a thermometer, a bucket lid tool, and a copy of "The Humanure Handbook.

This is a very basic composting toilet, but compared to the price of most commercial composting toilets ($1,500 and up), this unit is only $299.00 with free shipping anywhere in the US. It is another option you might want to check out, but keep in mind, it is "Basic.". You can obtain more information at Joseph Jenkins' website, at www. humanurehandbook.com.

If you are going to consider a commercial unit, you will need to determine how often it will be used by how many people, will it require power to run a fan, and is it legal to use one in your area. Although these units can be an option for those not wanting to be dependent on the local "system," or want to reduce the water required for a conventional sewer type system, you will need t do some homework. Make sure that they can provide for all your needs if you plan on using them full-time. If you are only going to use one as a temporary back-up system for your regular toilet, then a smaller, self-contained unit might be an option. Some of these units can use 12-Volt solar power to operate the exhaust fan, which is handy for those who have solar.

Staying Clean

Part of being self-reliant is being able to keep yourself, your clothes, and your home clean, without depending on power and stores for all your needs. Of course, you can still use your domestic clothes washers or dryers, but you should have an alternative to these devices in the event they are unusable. You should also have the supplies, that will allow you to make your own detergents, soaps, and cleaning agents. Let's take a look at some of the options that are available, that can be supplemental to the items you use regularly, can be used to replace your high energy use devices, or replace the expensive commercial cleaning agents you now use.

Making Your Own Laundry Detergent

If you use a regular washer for your clothes, one way you can reduce the cost of doing so is to make your own laundry detergent. The price keeps going up and you can make it with a few simple ingredients and it works as well as store bought, and even works in washers that require High Efficiency detergent. Our detergent costs fourteen cents (14¢) per load versus twenty-six cents (26¢) per load with store bought detergent.

My wife, Denise, has been researching and experimenting with various mixtures for laundry detergent, as well as other cleaning agents, and this is the laundry detergent we now use exclusively.

The ingredients and equipment needed for making your own laundry detergent are very basic. In regard to equipment, you will need a hand grater, or to make the process faster, a small food processor or blender. My wife purchased a small Grundig Hand Blender at Amazon.com for $39.99 for the exclusive use of making soap and detergent (there are cheaper and more expensive models). By having a small blender dedicated for this use, we don't have to use the one we use for food.

Next you will need the ingredients, and if possible, buy them in large bulk packs as it brings the price down even more. You will need Borax, Arm & Hammer Washing Soda, Oxy Clean (optional), and a bar of Fels-Naptha Soap.

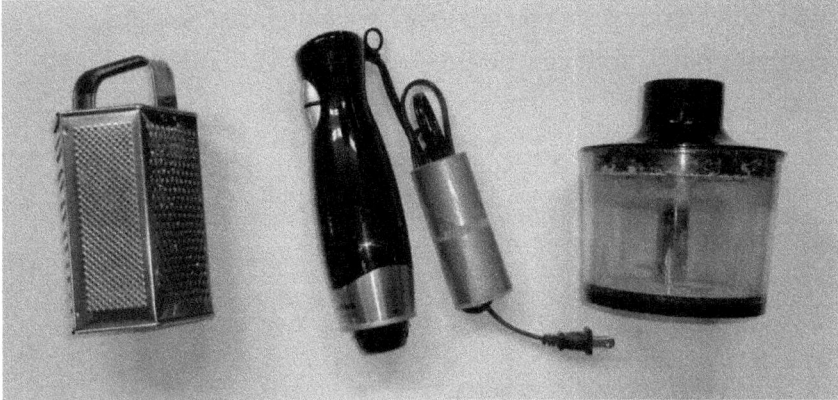

The above photo shows a Hand Grater on the left and a small Hand Blender in the center and right.

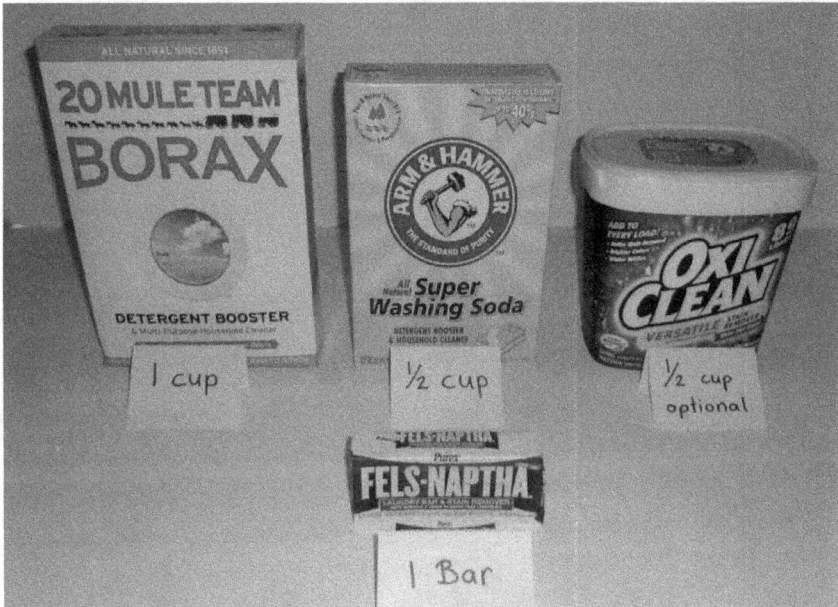

The above photo shows the ingredients required to make your own laundry detergent and the amount used per batch. It even works in washers that require High Efficiency detergent.

First, you must process the bar of Fels-Naptha soap. If you have a food processor or blender, you will first need to cut the bar into small pieces so they can be inserted into the food process or blender. You will then process the soap in the device until it is small and crumbly. If you are using a hand Grater, use the smallest grating surface, and process the bar until it is small and crumbly.

When using a food processor or blender, the bar of Fels-Naptha first has to be cut into small chunks.

Use a Hand Blender to process the soap until small and crumbly.

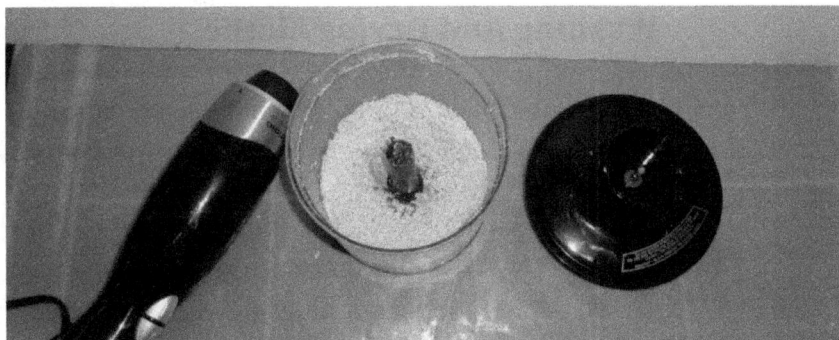

This is what the bar of Fels-Naptha soap should look like when it is completely processed, either with a Grater, Food Processor, or Blender. It should be small and crumbly.

After processing the bar of Fels-Naptha soap, you take one (1) cup of Borax, one-half (1/2) cup of Arm & Hammer Washing Soda, and one-half (1/2) cup of Oxy Clean (the Oxy Clean is optional but we find it makes the detergent work better), and mix these ingredients with the processed soap bar. You can do this in the blender or food processor, or if you don't have these, you can mix all the ingredients together well using a spoon or whisk.

This shows what the completed laundry detergent should look like.

When you have completed your laundry detergent, you should store it in a tightly sealed container. We have used a one quart canning jar and a 16 oz. "Deli-Container."

Washing And Drying Clothes

Now that you have made your own laundry detergent, you can use it in your washing machine. But what if the power goes out and you still need to wash and dry clothes?

You can always use a two-bin sink, such as those often found in a kitchen. Use one side for washing, and the other side for rinsing. This type of sink is normally small, so you will have to do small loads. Once the clothes have been rinsed, ring them out well.

An item that will make washing easier is an item called the Breathing Hand Washer, which is made in the U.S. and is sold by Lehman's. It is a device that looks like a plunger, but it has plastic baffles that sends water rushing through clothes to flush out dirt. This device also works well for simply washing clothes in a five gallon bucket.

There is also a device called the Rapid Laundry Washer, which does the same thing, but is made from Tin Plated Steel. My good friend's the Gregersen's have had problems with it rusting, and they now prefer the plastic Breathing Hand Washer. Whichever you choose, they will make the job of hand washing much easier.

If you really want to be self-reliant, then make your own five gallon bucket washer using a plunger. All you need is a five gallon bucket, a snap-on/snap-off lid, and a basic plunger. What I mean by a basic plunger is one that does not have a fold-out flange for using with toilets. I had a hard time find a basic plunger, as all the ones at Home Depot had the fold out flange. However, these type of plungers are heavy duty, so I purchased one and just cut the flange off with a knife. Now I had a basic plunger.

The above shows the three parts you will need to make a five gallon bucket clothes washer. A five gallon bucket, a snap-on/snap-off lid, and a plunger.

If your plunger has a fold out flange, simply cut it off.

You will need to drill a one inch hole in the center of the lid, for the handle of the plunger to fit through.

Drill a one inch hole in the lid for the plunger handle to fit through.

Next you need to drill holes in the head of the plunger. If you don't, when you push down on it in the water, it will just suction the clothes. You want the water to be forced through the clothes, pushing the dirt out. I drilled eight 1/4 inch holes in the head of the plunger.

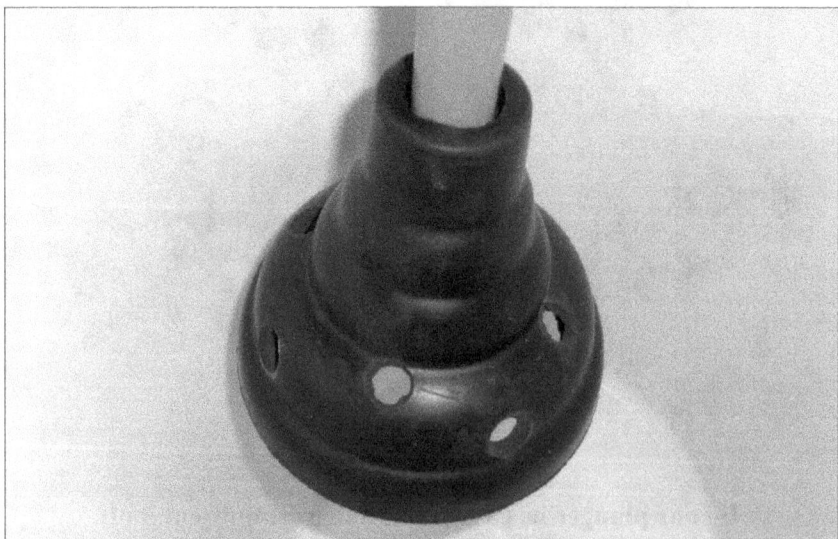

Four 1/4 inch holes were drilled around the top of the plunger, and four 1/4 inch holes offset on the sides.

I have seen various configurations, but many that I have seen only drill holes in the top. I drilled four in the top, then alternated four in the side, off-set from those in the top. I felt this would better agitate the water through the clothes, as water could squirt straight up, and also through the sides. I can't scientifically prove this is better, but it works well. It should be note, that if the flange had not been cut-off then the water would not be able to squirt through the holes in the plunger.

You now simply fill the bucket half full of warm water, add a small amount of detergent, place the plunger in the bucket, and place the lid on the bucket, with the plunger handle sticking up through the hole.

The above shows the five gallon bucket clothes washer ready to go.

I push the plunger up and down on the clothes for three to four minutes. I then empty the dirty water and wring the soap out of the clothes. I replace with fresh water and plunger again to rinse. I then wring the clothes out again and hang to dry.

This shows how the plunger agitates the detergent in the water. The cover was removed for the photo, but should be on the bucket when pressing the plunger up and down.

I'm sure you have all heard of a washboard, and this will also work for cleaning clothes. However, it is my understanding that they are rough on clothes, wearing them out quicker, as well as your hands. We keep one around for really tough dirt on items, but the Breathing Hand Washer is a preference.

If you planned on washing clothes by hand for any length of time, I would suggest that you get some galvanized wash tubs. Lehman's sells some made for this purpose and they hold 15.5 gallons. They also have a twin-tub arrangement with a heavy frame that holds them together. This provides one for washing and one for rinsing. Another handy item is a hand ringer. I remember using one of these as a child, helping my mother do laundry. It is basically two rollers in a frame. You simply feed the rinsed clothes between the two rollers while turning the hand crank, removing more water from them than a spin-dryer on a washer.

This shows Susan Gregersen washing clothes using a two wash tub system. A hand wringer can be seen mounted between the two tubs, and a Rapid Laundry Washer can be seen lying across the first galvanized tub. Photo by Steve Gregersen

Once your clothes have been washed and wrung out, they will need to be hung up to dry. When I was young, we had a clothesline that stretched from our house to the back garage. It was a doubled line, with a pulley on each side, whereby you had one continuous line. As you pushed one line out, the other came back towards you. You could stand by the house, and as you hung a piece of clothes, you simply pushed it out towards the garage When the clothes were dry, you could keep pulling them towards you in order to retrieve them.

A clothesline can be hung most anywhere, even on the balcony of an apartment. I have even seen clotheslines between alleys using the pulley system described in the previous paragraph. Again, innovation and imagination comes in handy here. Nothing smells better than clothes that have been dried outside.

Another handy device for drying clothes, if you have even a small piece of property, is the collapsible "umbrella" clothesline. This item requires that you place a small pipe into the ground to insert the "umbrella" into. This pipe comes with the collapsible clothesline and usually has an insert to perfectly fit the outside diameter of the clothesline pole. Once you place the pole into the pipe, you open it like an umbrella and you have a clothesline for drying your clothes.

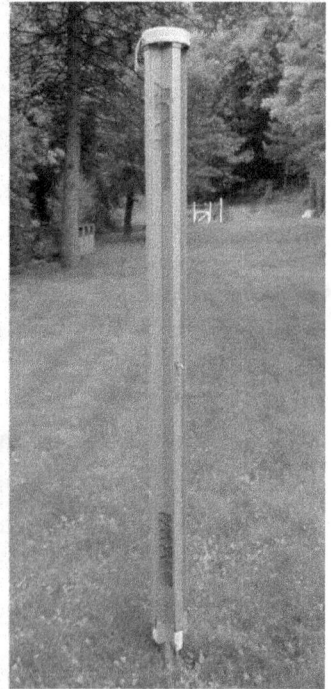

The left photo above shows the author inserting the collapsible umbrella clothes drying rack into the pipe holder in the ground. The right photo shows it inserted and ready to open.

This shows the author's collapsible umbrella clothesline in the up position. It collapses down and can be taken out of the ground tube and stored inside.

Of course, if the weather is bad outside, either being rainy or freezing, you will have to hang your clothes inside. Again, with some imagination, you should be able to string up a clothes line of some sort in order to hang the clothes for drying.

There is a device called a "Retractable Clothesline" that can be mounted on a wall, and a hook placed on the opposite wall. This is similar to a clothesline that is often available in the shower at a hotel. When you need to use it, you simply pull the line out and attach it to the opposite wall using the hook. When your clothes are dry, you simply unhook it, and it retracts back into its reel. The ones I have seen can pivot sideways, against the wall, when not in use, taking up little space.

Another great way to dry clothes inside is by using a collapsible folding floor dryer. They come in various sizes and Lehman's has some nice ones that are Amish-made. I have the medium sized one and it is very handy when you need to dry some clothes inside. When you are not using it, it collapses down, onto itself, making a compact package for storage.

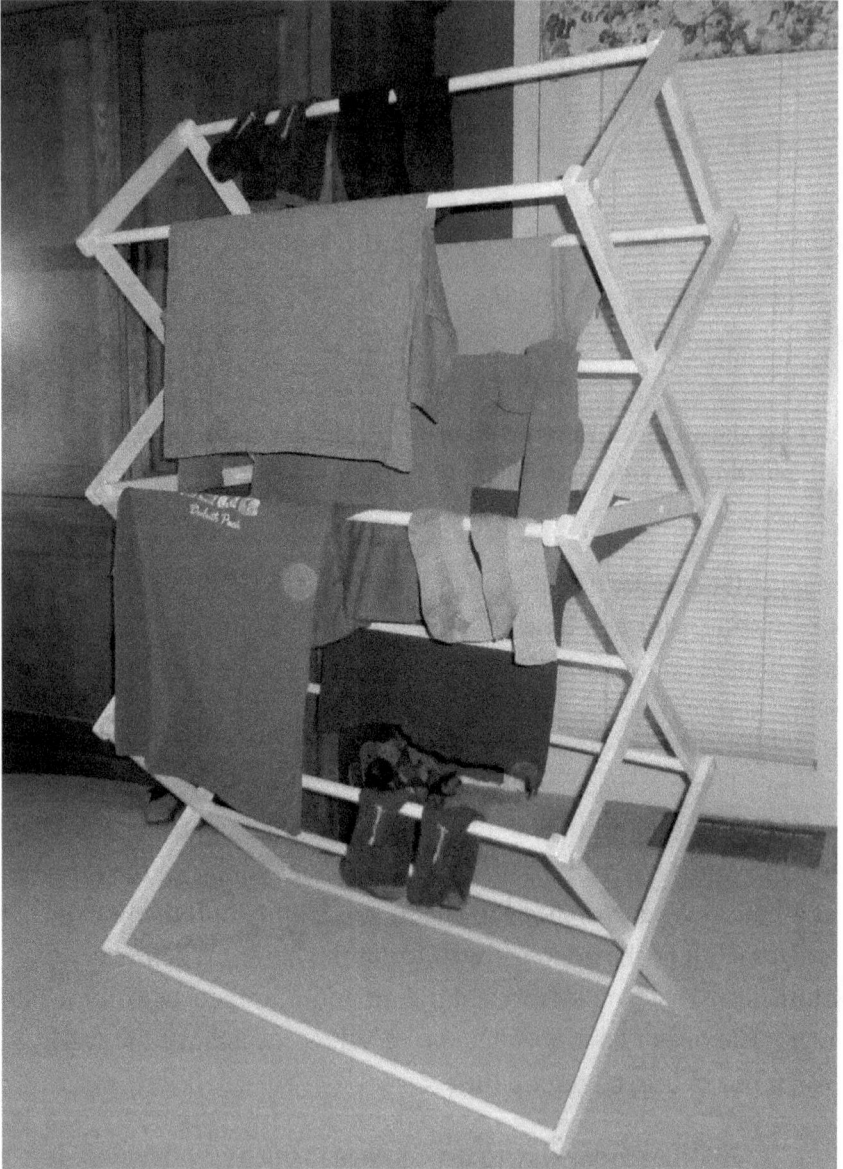

This photo shows the author's collapsible folding floor dryer.

If you have forced air heat, this collapsible clothes dryer works rather quickly when placing it in front of a heat register.

Making Soap

Making your own soap is the starting point for cleaning agents. Some cleaning agents that will be discussed later will use soap that you have made. First of all, I will state right up front, the actual making of soap is beyond the scope of this book, as there are many intricacies involved. However, I will point you in the right direction in regard to where to find the necessary information, and some pointers that will help you along the way.

My wife does the soap making in our house (although I am allowed to help), and she has checked out many books. The one she recommends to get you started is "Basic Soap Making" by Patsy Buck. This book is available at SurvivalResources.com.

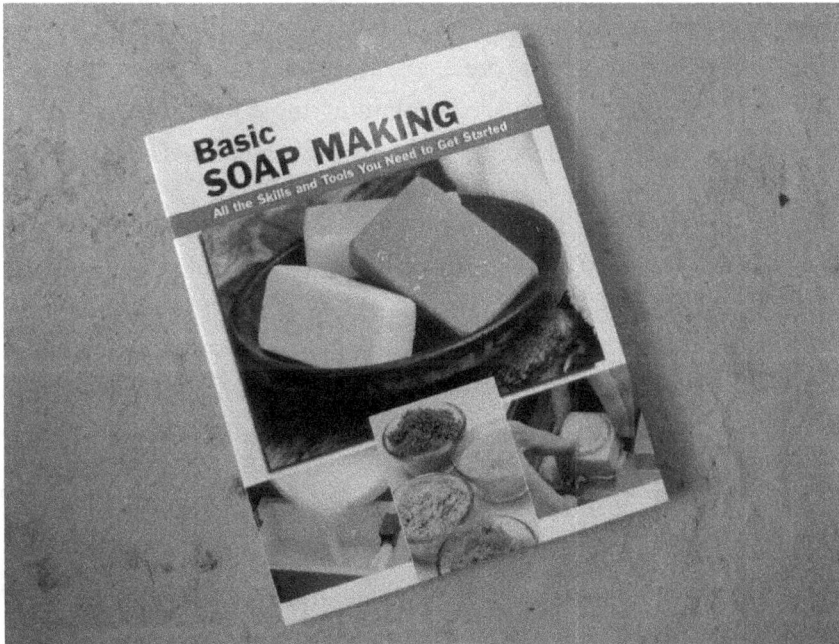

This shows the cover of the book "Basic Soap Making" which is the recommended book to get started making soap.

Some of the tools and supplies you need are plastic or glass containers, a thermometer, a good quality accurate scale, various spatulas and whisks, made from rubber, silicone or stainless steel. Because of the caustic nature of one of the main ingredients , lye, you will need some protective gear, to include rubber gloves, safety goggles, a face mask (such as a N95 protective mask), and an apron or something to protect your clothes, and you should wear long sleeves to protect bare arms.

The basic ingredients you will need are any liquid or solid oil, such as olive oil, Canola, sunflower, oil or Crisco or coconut oil. You will also need distilled water (see Chapter 10 for making your own distilled water) and 100% lye.

The amount of the contents you use varies greatly depending on the oils you use. The process requires accurate measuring of components, precise temperatures for mixtures, and a lot of stirring. As you can see, explaining the entire process here would take up too much room, but here are some hints.

Lye Is Caustic!, so be very careful when handling it. When it comes in contact with bare skin it can cause chemical burns, scarring, and blindness if you get it in your eyes. When mixed with water, it becomes hot, which can burn you. You need the mask, and a well ventilated area, because the chemical reaction it creates causes fumes. As you can see, lye is not something to play around with.

An immersion blender (this is a small hand-held blender that can be placed down into the bowl) will make stirring the mixture much easier.

There are various types of molds you can use. From a simple wooden box lined with wax paper to ones commercially available. Some molds are large, and require that you cut the bars of soap off a large block. My wife prefers silicone baking pans, as they are flexible, which makes it easy to get the soap out of, and you can find some that replicate the shape of store purchased soap.

This is a view of a silicone baking mold that the author's wife uses as a soap mold, which makes it easy to get the soap out.

It should be noted that, once the soap is completed, it has to cure for approximately a month before you can use it. You take it out of the mold and set it on a plastic screen for air drying, which cures the soap.

This shows completed soap curing on plastic screen.

Making soap is not difficult, but it is something that you have to take your time with, and work in a precise manner. Success depends on the accuracy of your mixtures and temperatures.

Making Cleaning Agents.

Making your own cleaning agents is another way you can reduce your dependency on store bought products, and save yourself a lot of money at the same time. We make most of our own cleaning agents and they can be made with a few ingredients. They work as well, if not better, than those touted as being the best for particular purposes. The photograph below shows the simple ingredients that we use to make our own cleaning agents.

The above photo shows the various ingredients for making household cleaning agents. Back row, from left to right shows Borax, Ammonia, Rubbing Alcohol, Vinegar, and Distilled Water. The front row on left shows homemade bar soap and Glycerin.

These are our favorite home-made cleaning mixtures:

Window Cleaner

1 part - Rubbing Alcohol
10 parts - Distilled Water
10 Parts - Vinegar

Dish Soap

        1-3/4 - Cups Boiling Distilled Water

        1 - Tablespoon Borax

        1 - Tablespoon Grated Bar Soap

All Purpose Cleaner

        2 - Tablespoons Ammonia

        1 - Teaspoon Dish Detergent (made above)

        2 - Cups Rubbing Alcohol

Shampoo

        3 - Cups Distilled Water

        3 - Cups of Soap Flakes or Grated Bar Soap

        8 - Teaspoons Glycerin

As the above illustrates, making your own cleaning agents can be accomplished with a few basic ingredients that can be purchased in bulk, which reduces the cost even more. They are simple to make and will provide you with a sense of satisfaction, knowing you have added one more feather in your hat of self-reliance.

Solar Showers

Solar showers were designed for use when camping, but they can be a handy item around the house as well. Basically they are a large black water bag that has a small shower head attached at the bottom. The ones we have are five gallon, and you simply fill them with water and set them in the sun. In a couple of hours you have warm to hot water to shower with.

What I like about these type of showers are they can be used even by people who live in the city, an apartment, etc.

Simply fill and hang outside a south facing window, or on a balcony. Once the water is hot, you can take it and hang it in your regular shower and shower as normal. If you are in the country, you can actually set up some poles and wrap a tarp around them. You now have a warm weather, outdoor shower.

We have two, one being a five gallon Seattle Sports, and another five gallon made by Texsport, which has four mesh pockets on the front for shower accessories. They are handy when the power goes out and can be stored in very little space under the bathroom sink. You might want to consider getting one to have on hand, just in case.

The author showing a five gallon solar shower made by Seattle Sports. Fill it with water and let the sun heat the water.

Sanitation and Hygiene are important aspects of life and can't be ignored. By following some of the suggestions in this chapter you will be less dependent on others. If only for emergency situations, you will be better prepared to take care of your own needs.

Chapter 14
<u>Staying Warm & Cool</u>

In this chapter we will discuss various ways that will help you to keep yourself warm and cool, depending on the season and temperature. Unfortunately, heating and cooling often start with the design of your home, and in many cases for those who live in an apartment or condominium, you have no control over the design features.

For this reason, I will start with something that anybody can do, no matter where they live. A while back, I purchased a book called "Movable Insulation - A Guide to Reducing Heating and Cooling Losses Through the Windows In Your Home" by William K. Langdon, and I found it very interesting.

This book provides a multitude of ways that you can build and use insulation panels to reduce heating and cooling losses through the windows of your home. As indicated, you can use these ideas no matter where you live, because you don't have to modify your home, which is especially helpful if you don't own it.

Moveable Insulation

A typical residence will lose 25 to 30% of its heat through windows. If you have large windows or sliding glass doors, you may lose up to 50% or more. All windows are poor insulators, even double pane, and you can lose 10 times more heat through a window than a well insulated wall of the same size. We tend to insulate walls, but not windows.

The book "Movable Insulation" provides a lot of information and suggestions for insulating your windows in the winter, and also using insulation to help cool your house in the summer. Although there are a plethora of ideas, I only experimented with a few that I thought could be used by anyone.

This shows the book, "movable Insulation" which is very unique and provides ideas for reducing heating and cooling losses through windows. These ideas can even be used by those who live in an apartment or condo.

Of course, there is a section on curtains, and even if you live in an apartment, they can be your first line of defense against cold, and heat. Long heavy curtains, when drawn in the winter can reduce heat loss through your windows at night. During the day, the curtains on the south side can be opened to allow the sun's rays to enter your house and help keep it warm. This is an ongoing process, of opening and closing, but it does help control heat loss, and gain.

Curtains also can help in the summer. Close them during the day on the south side and you block the heat from the sun entering the room. At night, open them, as well as the windows, to allow the cool air to circulate.

One of the interesting parts of the book deals with using light insulative panels, directly on the windows to insulate them from the cold. I tried a couple of the configurations and they are easy to build and do insulate the windows.

The first I tried are called "Friction-Fit Pop-In Shutters. These are easy to make using very lightweight insulation panels. I purchased a few panels of DOW® Super Tuff-R Insulation in 1/2 inch thickness, which has an R-Value of 3.3, at Home Depot.

Although this is a simplification of the technique for this type of set-up , you basically cut the insulation board to friction fit inside the window frame, inside your house. You then use small toggles to hold it in place. I tried it on one window and you could tell that less cold emminated through that window area than others, that did not have the insulation attached. The insulation value of the panel would also prevent the conduction of the warmth inside, through the window to the outside.

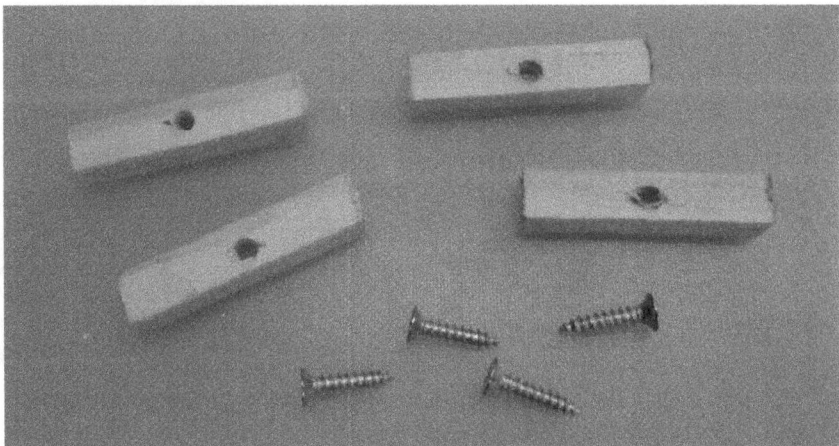

This shows the small wooden toggles the author made to hold the insulation panel within the window frame.

This photo shows an insulation panel cut to size and installed inside a window frame. Small wooden toggles hold it in place.

This is a close-up of the wooden toggles to hold the insulation panel in place.

In the experiment above, the insulation panel is not directly up against the window, but a couple, to a few inches, from it, depending on the depth of the window frame. According to the book, the closer the insulation panel is to the window, the more effective it is. My next experiment was with the "Glass-Hugging Pop-In Shutters." This technique places the insulation panels directly onto the windows.

The insulation panels are cut to the actual size of the glass, not including the frame. Then using flexible magnetic self-sticking, strips on both the panel and the glass, you basically stick an insulation panel directly to each glass panel

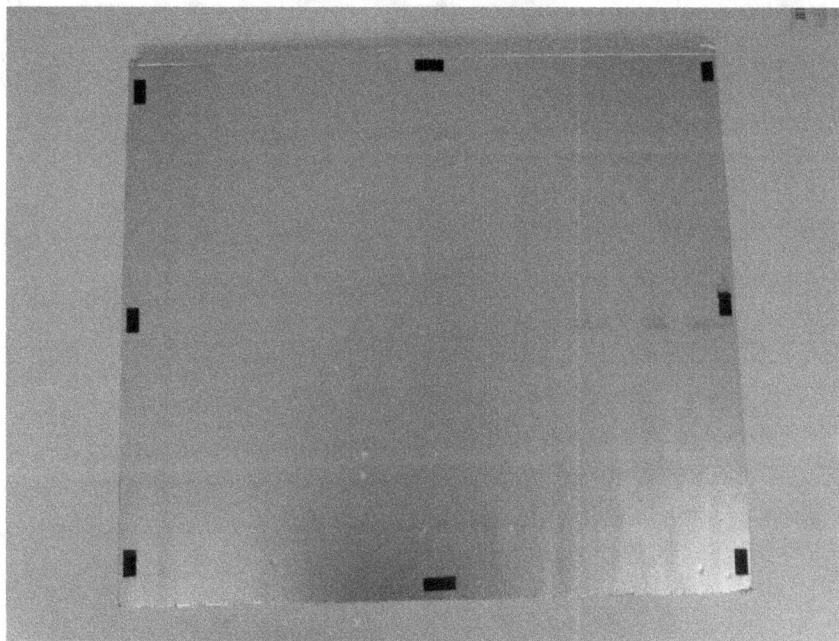

This shows the shiny backside, of the insulation panel with the magnet strips stuck in place.

I must admit, I only tried one half of a large window, just to see if the covered panel was warmer on the inside than the glass panel. Again, the insulation value of the panel would also prevent the conduction of the warm inside air to the outside.

This photo shows the matching magnets stuck to the window. a white board was held up outside of the window to get this photo.

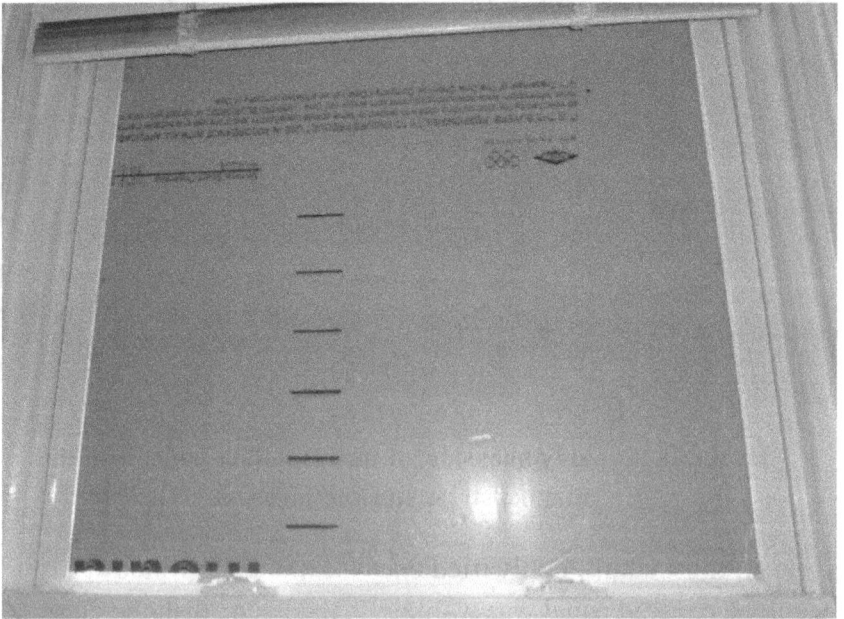

This photo shows the insulation panel held directly onto the glass window pane with the magnets.

The inside of the bare glass panel was cold. The inside of the glass with the insulation panel on it was considerable less cold. This would indicate, at least to me, that there would be less cold entering the room through the glass with the insulation panel, and less conduction of heat out of the room.

This technique has some draw-backs, at least in my mind. First, it is a lot more work. Cutting panels for each actual window pane, attaching magnets to each panel and window, and then storing all these small panels, as opposed to several large panels.

Of course, neither of these experiments were very scientific in nature, and an entire room would have to be done, measurements taken with and without the panels, etc. I ran by the seat of my pants on this one, yet in my opinion, the panels have merit, and can help prevent heat loss from a room through windows. If long heavy drapes have been proven to do so, these panels definitely can't hurt. I have included it here only as another option for preserving what heat you have.

It should be noted, that these panels can also be useful in the summer in your south and west facing windows. The reflective side facing out will help reflect the sun's rays out of the room, as well as shade the inside of the room. Just something else to think about.

There are many more ideas in regard to reducing heating and cooling losses through your windows in this book. If you are interested in this further, I recommend that you buy it.

Shutters and Overhangs

Shutters used to be common on homes until the mid 1800's. During the winter, people would open and close these shutters daily to help seal the residence from cold and wind. They also used louvered interior shutters in warmer climates to screen out summer heat. But when cheap fossil fuel, like coal, came into use, for central heating, shutters were discontinued and became just an ornament. Then, years later when air conditioning was introduced, even sun-shading shutters began to disappear.

When I was young we had awnings over all the south and west facing windows. In the summer, they would be extended out so that they would shade the windows from the direct rays of the sun. This helped to shade those windows so the sun did not directly enter the rooms, keeping them cooler. Awnings today don't seem to be as prevalent as they once were.

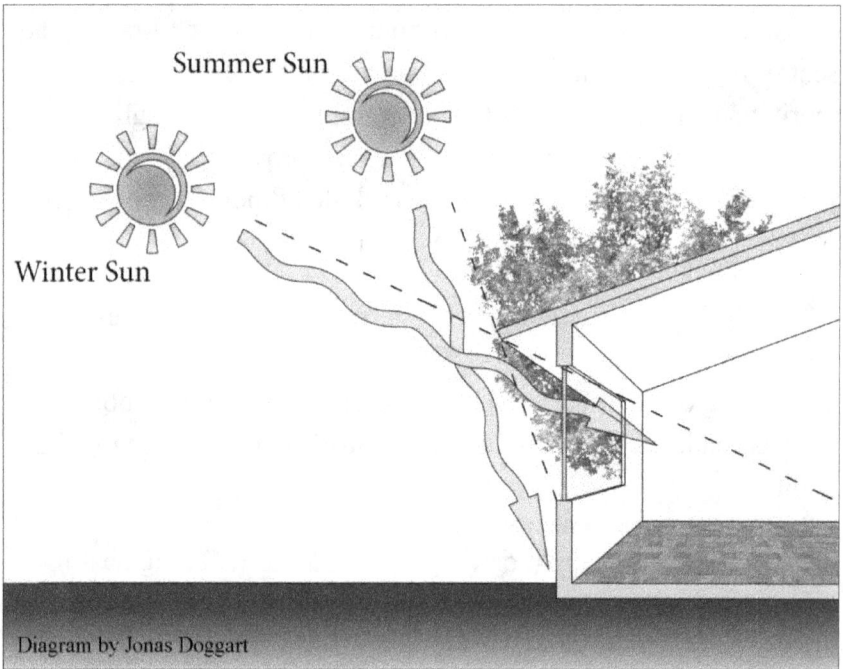

Diagram by Jonas Doggart

The above diagram shows the advantage of an overhang on a house. It blocks the high summer sun from entering, but will allow the lower winter sun to enter, for additional warmth.

Overhangs on houses are another way to control the sun's rays from entering your house, which as we know creates heat. If you live in a residence that you cannot modify, then there is not much you can do with building overhangs. But if you can modify your residence, then overhangs serve dual purpose. In the summer, when the sun is high, a properly designed overhang can restrict direct ray's of the sun from entering your house. Yet in the winter, when the sun is lower, it will allow the sun's rays to enter, providing additional free heat.

If you cannot modify your structure, such as an apartment, etc. you can still control the amount of the sun's rays that enters your south and west facing windows. You can simply add roll down shades, or venetian blinds. They can be raised and lowered to the height you want, and with the venetian blinds, you can angle them to block the sun, but yet allow ventilation through an open window.

Passive Solar

The use of shutters and overhangs as described in the above section are actually Passive Solar techniques. If you do own your own home, or plan to do so, then one of the better books I have found on this subject is called "The Solar House - Passive Heating and Cooling" by Daniel D. Chiras.

This book goes in depth with the Fundamentals of Integrated Passive Design, Solar Heating & Solar Cooling for specific regions, Supplying Back-Up Heat Sustainably, Health Matters: Optimum Air Quality in Passively Conditioned Homes, Designing a Passively Conditioned Home and Assessing Its Performance.

I have found this book to be a great resource with a lot of information, photos, and diagrams. If you plan on modifying or building your own home, and want to incorporate passive solar techniques, this would be a good book to have.

This is a good book to learn the fundamentals and design features of passive heating and cooling.

One of the things I found very interesting in this book was the use of a Thermal Mass to collect the heat from the sun, store it, and then reradiate it at night. This is considered a Direct-Gain method, which relies on south-facing windows to permit sunlight to enter during the heating season, whereby it is converted to heat inside the living space, heating it directly.

I cannot do this subject justice in such a short space as this section, but the following will explain Thermal Mass collection in regard to its use in a residence to collect and reradiate heat. I thank my step-son, Jonas, for his ability to make me diagrams that shows this concept.

Basically, thermal storage works best when nighttime heating is the primary goal. A thermal mass prevents overheating and stores heat, which is released passively when the temperatures fall below the mass surface temperature.

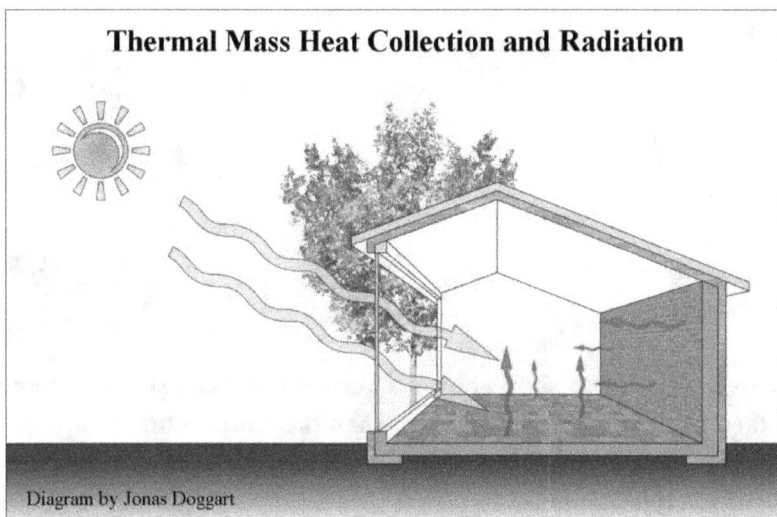

This diagram shows how a Thermal Mass can store heat and then reradiate it into the room when the temperature drops at night.

The thermal mass must be able to collect and hold the heat from the sun. One of the ideas is to use a wall of brick or stone that will absorb the heat. Another idea I have also heard about, is using black water barrels as the wall, but it might be a difficult design feature. The diagram above shows a light colored stone floor, which will absorb and reflect heat to the brick, which will absorb and store the heat. When the temperature drops at night the heat will be reradiated back into the room.

Another design feature that can be utilized is the use of vents in the thermal mass wall to transfer heat to an adjoining room by natural convection. The lower vents draw cool air from the adjoining room, and heat rising will transfer through the upper vents into the adjoining room.

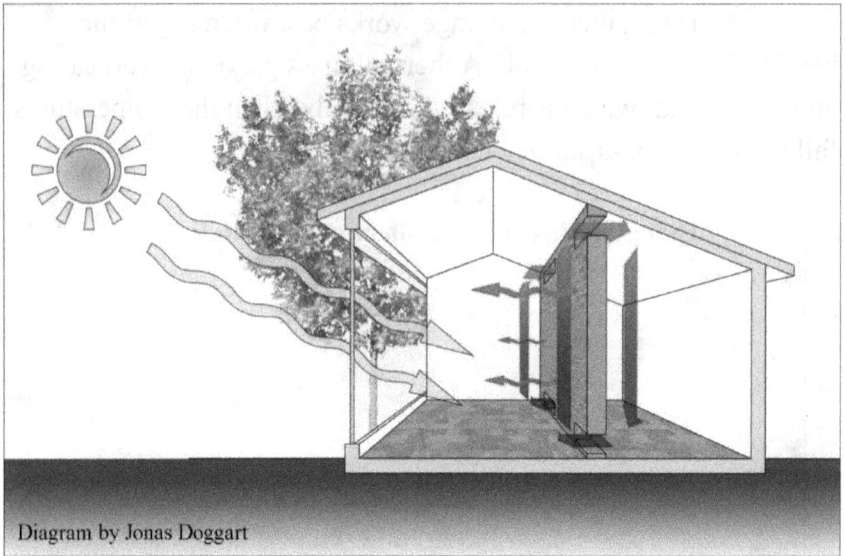

Diagram by Jonas Doggart

This diagram also shows how a Thermal Mass can store heat and then reradiate it into the room when the temperature drops at night. It also shows how vents in the upper and lower portion of the thermal mass can transfer heat to an adjoining room through convection.

Keep in mind, and this is my input, that with the above thermal mass heat collection and radiation, this would be a good time to utilize a means to cover the windows at night with one of the previous discussed methods of moveable insulation, even if just heavy drapes. If you don't cover the windows, the heat stored in the thermal mass will be lost through the windows to the outside through convection. Just my thought on the matter.

There is a lot of other information in the above mentioned book. It is a great resource if you are going to be buying a home, or building one yourself. I highly recommend it.

Solar Air Heating Systems

I know I have already mentioned a couple of good books in this chapter, but there are so many great books on this subject that you rarely hear about. There is one more I would like to address, and it is called "The Complete Handbook of Solar Air Heating Systems" by Steve Kornher with Andy Zaugg. This is a great book with a multitude of projects that you can build.

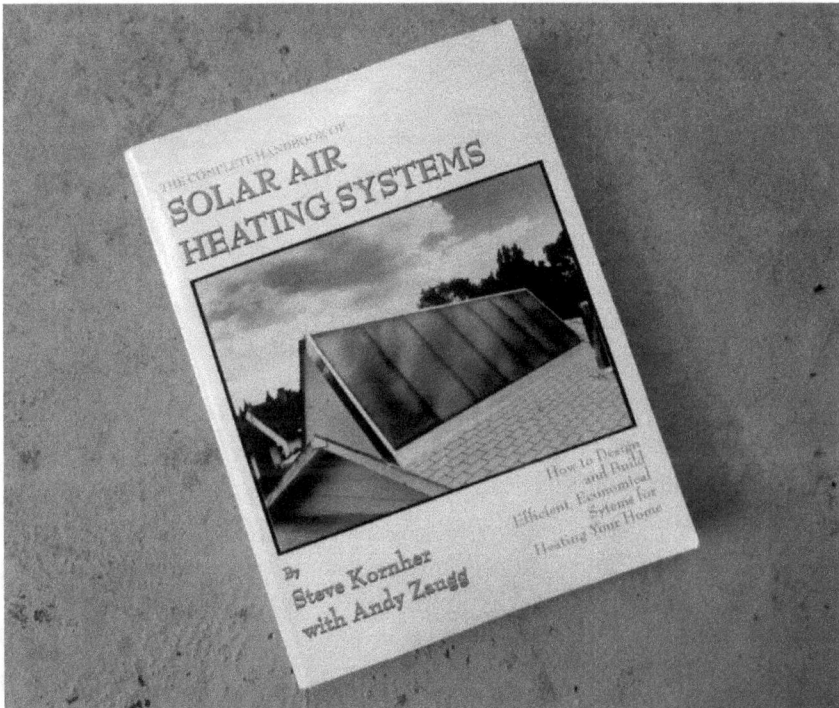

"The Complete Handbook of Solar Air Heating Systems" is a great book with a multitude of projects that you can build.

One of the projects in the book is the building of a Window Box Collector, which is a type of Convective Air Heater. This seemed like a project that someone with a little skill, and tools, could accomplish. There are two types, an Angled Vent, and a Straight Vent, Construction.

Window Box Collectors

Diagram by Jonas Doggart

This diagram shows the two types of Window Box Collectors, which are convective air heaters. The one on the left is an Angled Vent construction, and the one on the right is a Straight Vent construction.

Although the angled vent allows the window to close further when inserted through a window, it needs some flashing at the top to prevent the pooling of rain water on top. The straight vent does not need this flashing, but takes up more space in the window, limiting the use of the entire bottom portion. This can be observed in the diagram on the previous page.

As mentioned, a window box collector is a convective air heater. It is mounted in a double hung window, and draws cool air from the room through the bottom chamber, where the air is heated in an upper chamber by the sun, via a glass window and a thermal mass. The warm air reenters the room via the top vent.

The book, described above, has a complete section describing in detail how to build a window box collector, with cross section diagrams. It provides parts required and how to put it together. I will briefly describe its construction, and show a side view, as well as a 3-D diagram, done by my step-son, Jonas Doggart.

This is very similar in construction to the angled collector on an Appalachian Solar Dehydrator (shown in Chapter 3 - Food Preservation), except the bottom end is closed. A flat box is constructed the width of the inside dimensions of a double-hung window. It is insulated on the bottom, bottom end, and sides. The bottom end of the box has a half round turning vane. There is a center divider providing two separate chambers, one on top and one on the bottom. The top of the box is made from a large piece of glass. The top chamber, uses metal lath, which is connected to the inside top glass side, at the top of the box. It then is angled down to the bottom of the center divider and connected there. The metal lath, painted black, acts as a thermal mass collecting the heat from the sun coming through the glass top. Being lath, it allows the air to travel through it as it is heated.

It is a little more complicated than this, as there are various construction details best shown in the book, which includes horizontal rods across the top chamber to hold the metal lath at an angle in the top chamber, the insertion of the turning vane at the inside bottom end, areas to caulk, etc. There are also details on how to properly mount the window box collector in the window frame. If you are interested in building one yourself, I suggest you buy the above mentioned book.

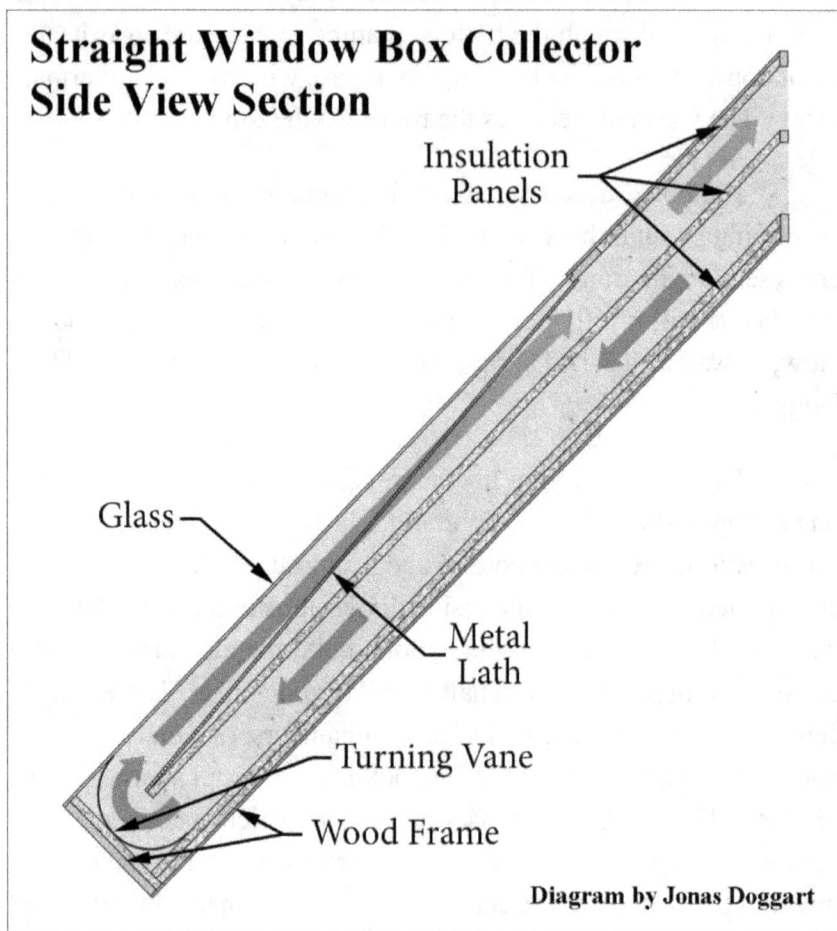

Straight Window Box Collector Side View Section

Insulation Panels

Glass

Metal Lath

Turning Vane

Wood Frame

Diagram by Jonas Doggart

This is a view of the window box collector constructed by the author's friend, Jim Tompkins, using the instructions from "The Complete Handbook of Solar Air Heating Systems."

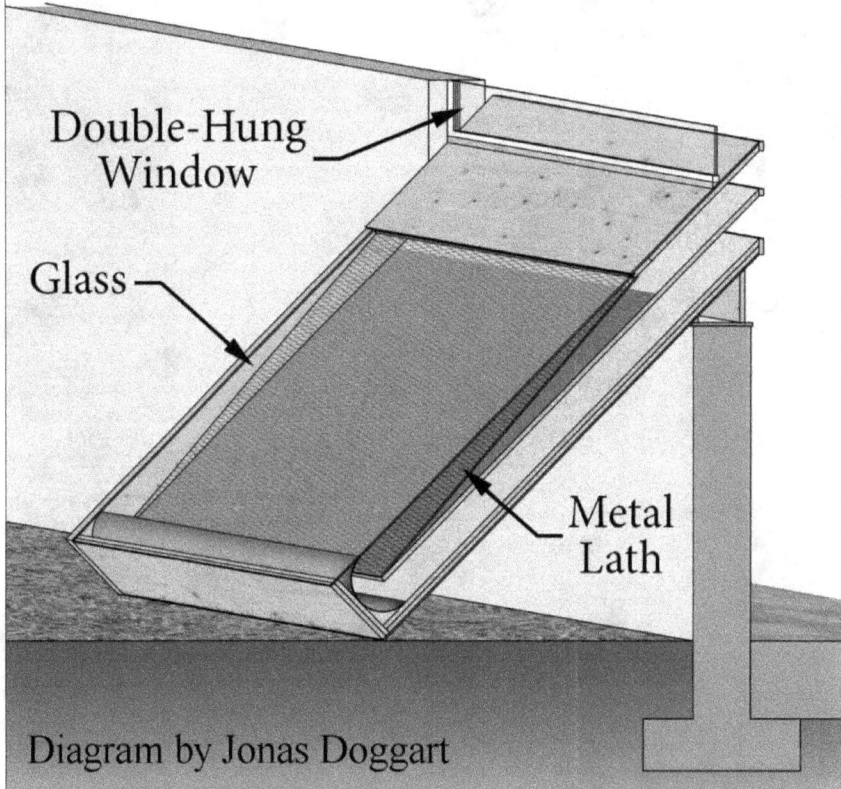

Straight Window Box Collector
3-D Sectional View

Double-Hung Window

Glass

Metal Lath

Diagram by Jonas Doggart

The above diagram shows a 3-D sectional view of a straight window box collector.

Although window box collectors are one of the simplest solar heating devices you can build, they are quite small in relation to the size of a room they are heating. Unless several are used, they won't provide a great percentage of the total heating needs. I still think they are neat, and any free heating by the sun is welcome.

I was going to build one of these, but my friend, Jim Tompkins beat me to it. He did an excellent job, and he was surprised that the heat that came out of the top chamber reached 100 degrees, in the middle of winter, when he had good sun.

This is a view of the window box collector constructed by the author's friend, Jim Tompkins, using the instructions from "The Complete Handbook of Solar Air Heating Systems."

There are many other projects in 'The Complete Handbook of Solar Air Heating Systems" and you just might want it in your reference library.

Solar Water Heating

Although this topic is not exactly about staying warm or cool, personally, it does need to be mentioned. Water can be heated by the use of solar power. It is another subject that could take a book itself, so I will only provide a brief outline

Basically, the amount of hot water that solar energy will provide depends on the type and size of the system, the climate, and the quality of the site in terms of solar access. A back-up heating system for water will often be necessary for those times when solar radiation is insufficient to meet your hot water demands. Solar water heaters come in a variety of shapes, sizes, and capabilities, ranging from small passive heaters to three- or four-panel active systems costing several thousand dollars.

The most common collector type used in domestic water heating, is a flat plate collector pane. The panel is an insulated weatherproof box containing a dark solar absorber plate under one or more transparent covers. It is the least expensive type collector.

This photo shows flat plate collector panels on a roof, which are the common collector type used for domestic solar water heating.

Some solar water heating systems use concentrating collectors instead of flat plate collectors. These collectors may be less effective during cloudy weather and are usually more expensive than flat plate systems. However, they can produce higher temperatures than flat plates. Another type of collector used for domestic water heating is the evacuated tube collector. These collectors consist of an absorber surface inside a tempered glass vacuum tube. The vacuum helps to reduce convective heat losses. The evacuated tube collector is the most expensive type.

This photo shows an evacuated tube collector which uses an absorber surface inside a tempered glass vacuum tube.

There are two common types of systems, being Passive or Active. In a Passive System you do not need a pump, and the water tank is situated horizontally above the heating panels. A pump is not required because the hot water will naturally rise into the tank through thermo-siphon (natural convection). The drawback to this type of system is that you need a strong roof structure to hold the weight of the water tank.

In an Active System, the water tank can be at ground level, but this requires an electric pump to force the water through the system. The obvious drawback to this system is, you need power.

SOLAR WATER HEATING

PASSIVE SYSTEM

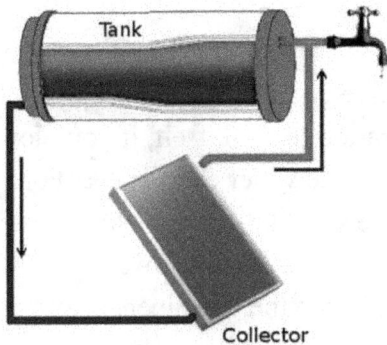

ACTIVE SYSTEM

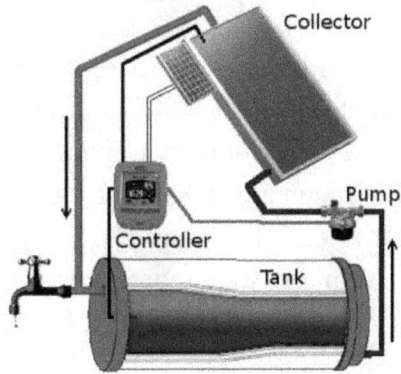

Collector

Tank

Collector

Pump

Controller

Tank

The above diagram shows, on left, a Passive solar water heating system whereby the water tank is mounted above the heating panels. The right side shows an Active system, whereby the water tank can be at ground level, but requires a pump to force water through the system.

There is much more information you would need before making a decision in regard to a commercial solar water heating system, and again, research or a consultant would be advisable.

There is also a solar water heater called the "Batch Water Heater" and it is the simplest of the solar hot water systems. It used to be called the "Breadbox" by the do-it-yourself community. Basically, it consists of a tank of water within a glass covered insulated enclosure aimed at the sun.

My good friend, Christopher Nyerges built one of these back in the late 1970s. In his book "The Self-Sufficient Home - Going Green & Saving Money" he explains how he built it and has both diagrams and photos. It is a good read.

Researching this type of solar water heater, I found that there is a multitude of DIYs on the internet. If interested, check them out for more details.

Evaporative Coolers

I have seen a lot of information lately on the internet with various plans for building evaporative coolers. The concept is simple, like our body using perspiration to cool itself, if you blow air through a wet material, it cools as the water evaporates. For many years at our survival camp, we would place a wet towel over the drinking water containers. We would keep the towel wet, and as the moisture evaporated, it would keep the containers of water cool.

What many people don't realize is that this method is only really effective in an area that has a low humidity. This is why they are often used in the southwestern region of the U.S., as the humidity level is below 30%. In the northeast we have humidity levels often in the 70-85% level, which makes the use of an evaporative cooler very ineffective.

If you live in a low humidity area, you may want to research various ways that an evaporative cooler might be useful for your cooling needs.

Conventional Heating & Cooling

There are many types of conventional heating and cooling methods, to include heat pumps, radiant floor heat, baseboard hot water systems, high-efficiency boilers and furnaces, wall-mounted space heaters, etc. However, the reliance on a fuel source, or electrical power, limits your ability to reduce your dependency on others. Unfortunately, most people will have to deal with some form of conventional heating or cooling system, especially if living on the grid. Obviously, an entire book could be written on various heating and cooling systems. I will only address a few that limit your dependency on fossil fuels.

Fireplaces

Although a nice fireplace, with a crackling fire, can be appealing, they are extremely inefficient, as most heat generated is lost up the chimney. In order to be useful, a fireplace insert is recommended, which is actually a wood stove which simply uses the chimney to exhaust gases. Fireplace inserts are much more efficient at heating than an open fireplace.

Wood Stoves

For the purpose of heating, a wood stove is a much better option than a fireplace. They come in a variety of sizes and styles and are widely available. They are easy to install and use, but they require wood to burn, which if you have to cut, haul, and split yourself, requires a lot of work. You also need access to the wood. There's an old adage that says firewood warms you twice: once when you cut it, and again when you burn it. Also keep in mind that you must tend to a wood stove, so when you are away from home, they won't be producing heat. Wood stoves usually work best in smaller homes, or to heat a particular room.

Pellet Stoves

I have heard pellet stoves called the lazy person's wood stove. Although easy to load, convenient, and automatic operation, they normally cost more than a wood stove and require electricity to operate fans and the auger.

I have a neighbor that bought one for when the power went out to heat the living room. However, now he has to keep a generator going when the power goes out, in order to run the fan and auger. I also have a friend who bought a multi-fuel pellet stove that also burns bio-fuels-such as corn, seeds, peanut shells, pits, etc., in addition to wood pellets. He indicates that the problem with pellets is demand. Dollar per BTU matches or exceeds all other commercially available heat sources when the demand is high.

Masonry heaters

Masonry heaters are wood burning stoves, but are made out of bricks and mortar. I find this type of heater is used more in Europe than in the U.S. My wife had one in her apartment in Switzerland when she was going to college and it heated the entire apartment.

They are designed to burn hotter than normal wood stoves and have a maze-like channel as part of the flue. This provides maximum heat transfer and accounts for its high efficiency at heating.

Conventional Cooling

Conventional cooling is basically limited to an air conditioner. About the best you can do is select the most energy efficient air conditioner you can find and run it in energy-saver mode. However, you will still be dependent on electrical power from the grid.

Chapter 15
__Transportation Options__

I saved this topic for last, because there is the least amount to say. When it comes to being self-reliant, transportation is a perplexing situation, because your options are very limited. The majority of transportation is based on fossil fuel, and the undeniable dependence on that fuel. It is difficult to reduce your dependency on something that is the normal mode of transportation.

One of the problems in the U.S., at least when you get out of the city, is everything is so spread out. The farther you get towards the country, the more spread out it gets. When I was younger, there were always small country stores that you could easily walk or ride a bike to. But because of malls and mega-stores, most of these little stores have been put out of business. No longer can I walk to a store for milk. It takes a trip.

Walking

In Switzerland, I am always amazed how few people have cars, and those that do, seldom use them. All towns, no matter how small, still have local stores and shops, and walking to a store is a normal activity. They also have sidewalks for walkers, even in the country. Once you get outside of an urban or suburban area in the U.S., sidewalks dry up and you're on the dirt shoulder of a country road, and vehicles find you as a nuisance that they must veer around.

I find that walking is not only healthy, but a means of transportation that the least amount of preparation, skill, or maintenance. As long as you keep up your energy level, you can travel. Of course, the problem is you can't get anywhere quickly, or travel very far in a short time span. Walking is, however, free.

Bicycles

Another form of transportation that only requires your own effort is a bicycle. Other than the maintenance on the bike (and of course yourself), you have a form of transportation that can get you somewhere relatively quickly, especially if compared to walking. However, once you get out of an urban area, it becomes more difficult to use a bike for transportation. Out in the country where I live, riding a bike on my road is taking your life into your own hands, and vehicles seem to consider you a hindrance to their travel. Not to bring up Switzerland again, but they have bike lanes everywhere. Even in the country, you can safely ride a bike without risking your life.

I do believe that when fossil fuel is either too expensive to buy, or is no longer available, a lot more people will be returning to the bicycle as a means of transportation.

For those who are concerned with "bugging-out" in the event of an emergency situation, a bicycle will be a viable option as is does not require fossil fuel, which will be difficult to impossible to obtain in such an occurrence.

I wanted to set up a bicycle for various emergency situations. It could be used during an electrical failure whereby getting gas from a gas station was not an option. During a longer term situation where I decided to Bug-In instead of Bug-Out, it could be used for travel, and have the ability to carry things on it. In the worst case scenario, whereby Bug-Out was necessary, it could be mounted to a vehicle and used as an alternate form of transportation. This bicycle would be a multi-purpose mode of transportation. It would have a rack on the front and back. It would have easily removable panniers for the rear, which could be used for something as simple as going shopping or carrying required gear for a Bug-Out. The panniers could be lifted off the rear rack with a carry handle and taken into camp, or wherever, for safe keeping.

I started with my Giant Yukon Se Mountain Bike. It is a 24 speed and has a "Roch Shok" front suspension system. The rear rack and panniers were no problem. It was the front that gave me a problem. When I was a kid, if you wanted a basket on the front, you mounted it to the handlebars and two support rods dropped down to the front wheel and where bolted over the wheel nuts. Simple and easy.

This is the author's bicycle that he modified for use as a mode of transportation in the event of a Bug-In or Bug-Out situation. Of course it can also be used as an everyday means of transportation.

With my mountain bike, there aren't any nuts on the wheels. They have a quick disconnect system in order to easily remove the wheels. The main problem was the front suspension system. You can't mount anything to the front wheel and the handlebars, because as you ride the bike, the front suspension goes up and down. The rack would have to be hinged and this would cause it to go up and down as you hit bumps. I wanted the rack stationary. I was successful at working around this problem by designing a special rack for the front. If you are interested in seeing how I built it, I have a complete article at SurvivalResources.com titled "Bug-In/Bug-Out Bicycle" which explains the building with many photos showing the process.

Animals For Transportation

Animals have been used for ages as a means of transportation. Humans have ridden them for transportation, used them as pack animals for carrying goods, and have harnessed them singly, or in teams, to pull sleds or wheeled vehicles.

How many people recall the older western movies, where everyone rode a horse, the settlers heading for California were in covered wagons, prospectors in the gold rush used mules to haul their supplies, stagecoaches were the means of cross-country travel, and a cart pulled by a horse was used to collect supplies from town. It was the normal mode of transportation.

With the advent of modern transportation, this mode of conveyance is rare, at least in the U.S. The Amish still rely on horses for transportation, but, unless you're out west, it is an exception to the rule. But in many countries, animals are still a typical means of transportation. Horses, mules, donkeys, oxen, buffalo, and camels are ridden and used to haul. In India, the bullock-cart (or ox-cart) is still the main means of transporting agricultural products. In Germany and Switzerland, I have seen wagons still being used as a means of transportation and to haul goods.

Part of the problem in modern society, is if it isn't motorized, it isn't considered a real means of transportation. The problem is not that animals cannot be used for transportation, but the perception of using them is outmoded.

This is a view of a woman in Germany using a horse and buggy as a means of transportation.

The downside of using animals for transportation is that they must be attended to. You cannot drive them home, park them in the garage, and wait for the next time you need to go somewhere. They must be fed, and you either have to grow, or buy the food. You must also take care of their health. If an animal gets hurt or sick, you must take care of that immediately.

Of course, motorized vehicles also require maintenance and repair, but it is not life threatening. And you are still reliant on fossil fuels.

Biodiesel

I hear a lot about biodiesel, but I have not been able to find anybody in my area that actually makes any. Biodiesel is a form of diesel fuel manufactured from vegetable oils, animal fats, or recycled restaurant greases. It is described as safe, biodegradable, and produces less air pollutants than petroleum-based diesel.

First of all, you must keep in mind that Biodiesel can only be used in a diesel engine. It does not work with regular gas engines, so that is a limiting factor if you drive a normal gas guzzler. Also, a required ingredient in biodiesel is lye, and we discussed the toxic nature of that component under "Soap Making" in Chapter 13. As with all fuel, you will need to be able to obtain in bulk, whatever you will be using to make the biodiesel, and a safe place to make the mixture.

I have not personally been involved with the making or using of biodiesel, nor do I have a great amount of knowledge on the subject. I plan on changing that position, but at this time, if you are further interested in the particulars involved, please research the topic thoroughly before attempting to make it.

Public Transportation

Whenever I read something about self-reliant transportation, I usually see public transportation listed. Although, in my opinion, public transportation is a means in which to limit your use of personal, fossil fuel required, vehicles, it is based on something that is provided by someone else, such as a government entity. This basically provides you with transportation that you do not have to provide, but you still have to pay for, and on which you still rely on someone else.

I'm not saying public transportation is not good. Although I must again refer to Switzerland, I am always amazed that there is nowhere I can't get to over there with public transportation. From a small town, to a suburb, to a city, or all the way to the Swiss Alps, public transportation is available. This is probably why so few need cars are needed.

Just keep in mind, that whether it be a bus, tram, train, or other form of public transportation, you are dependent on someone else, and their schedule. It can free you from having, and maintaining, your own vehicle, but it does not free you from dependence on others.

Chapter 16
<u>Final Thoughts</u>

There are many aspects of self-reliance, but you have to start somewhere. I believe the first step is the realization that you are far too dependent on others for your normal, everyday needs. The second step is to make a conscious decision to change that.

Self-reliance is not something that occurs overnight, but a slow, steady, progression. You start with those things you can easily, or readily, change or accomplish. Maybe start a small garden, even if it is on the balcony of an apartment. Growing some of the food you need is better than none.

Look at other things you can do. Recycle or repurpose things that you normally throw away. Try canning, even if you have to go to a farmers market to buy fruit and vegetables. When you buy things, try to buy a few extra and have a supply of those things that may be difficult to obtain, if you can't get out, lose your job, or other circumstance prevent you from doing so.

Try making your own soap or cleaning agents. Have an alternative means of lighting your house if the power goes out. Know that if it is cold you have a way to stay warm, and if it is hot, you can keep cool. These are all steps towards reducing your dependency on others for everything you need.

This brings us to debt. I'm not saying it is easy to get out of debt, but it can be done. Remember "Needs vs. Wants' and you will be spending less on things that you might only want, but don't actually need.

Ignore the "entitlement" proclamation you hear on every other television or radio commercial. Accept the fact that you are only entitled to what you produce or earn. There is no such thing as a "Free Lunch" as, ultimately, somebody pays for it. And when you hear that something is "Government Funded," remember it is therefore funded by you, the taxpayer.

The road to self-reliance is paved with stones you need to build your own life without depending on others for everything. Don't travel the road blindly, but be aware of those small pieces that you can grasp, and use, to build your own life free of dependency. At this point, it is up to you.

As I often say, "Being self-reliant is not a pastime, but a way of life." Hopefully I have provided some guidance with this book that will help you in your journey.

About the Author

John D. McCann is a true advocate of self-reliance. He practices the skills and works at a self-reliant lifestyle. He dislikes the term "Expert" and considers himself a student of self-reliance, survival, and emergency preparedness. He continues in his endeavor to learn and practice the skills necessary to enhance his knowledge and abilities.

John is the author of two previous books, "Build the Perfect Survival Kit," now in its 2nd Edition, and "Stay Alive! Survival Skills You Need." He has written dozens of articles and has been published in "Field and Stream," "Wilderness Way," where he was featured on the cover, "Self-Reliance Illustrated," and "Survival Quarterly Magazine." He has appeared on the "Martha Stewart Show" teaching how to build a survival kit. He also has various YouTube videos teaching skills.

He is the founder and owner of Survival Resources, a company that designs and builds custom survival kits, and sells products related to survival and emergency preparedness. He can be contacted at SurvivalResources.com

About the Author

Other Books By The Author

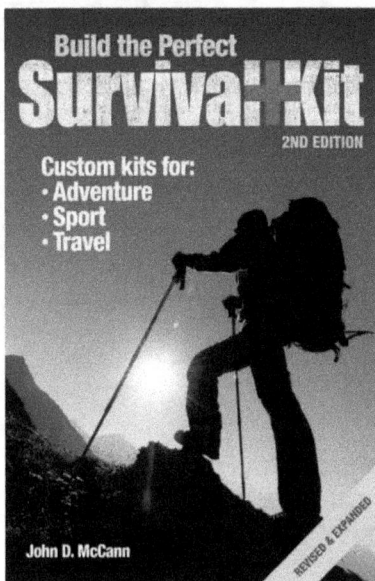

Build the Perfect Survival Kit is the first book ever written exclusively on building survival kits. It was published by Krause Publication (now KP Books), April, 2005. It was so successful that the publisher asked that he do a 2nd, Expanded and Revised Edition. It has a new Forward by Christopher Nyerges. With major additions to the components section and new chapters on Cookware & Stoves, Modifying Your Gear, Everyday Carry & Get-Home Bags, and Evacuation Kits & Bug-Out Bags. The 2nd Edition is 30% larger than the original.

Having a survival kit is not enough - You must know what to do with it! Armed with the techniques in **Stay Alive! Survival Skills You Need**, you will be prepared to survive. Building on the essentials presented in his first book, **Build the Perfect Survival Kit**, author John D. McCann details the survival mentality required to survive common emergencies, then goes on to explain the component skill categories that you must execute to stay alive. With more than 250 pages, 300 full-color photos, and a Foreword by Dave Canterbury, **Stay Alive! Survival Skills You Need** provides clear, detailed solutions for surviving emergencies during adventure, sport and travel.

www.ingramcontent.com/pod-product-compliance
Lightning Source LLC
Chambersburg PA
CBHW062158270326
41930CB00009B/1580